2009

D0460901

Chicken Salad, page 22

Cooking Light.

Salad

Oxmoor
House.

©2007 by Oxmoor House, Inc.
Book Division of Southern Progress Corporation
P.O. Box 2262, Birmingham, Alabama 35201

ISBN-13: 978-0-8487-3159-5
ISBN-10: 0-8487-3159-X
Library of Congress Control Number: 2006908792
Printed in the United States of America
First printing 2007

Be sure to check with your health-care provider before making any changes in your diet.

Oxmoor House, Inc.
Editor in Chief: Nancy Fitzpatrick Wyatt
Executive Editor: Katherine M. Eakin
Copy Chief: Allison Long Lowery

Cooking Light Salad
Editor: Terri Laschober Robertson
Nutrition Editor: Anne C. Cain, M.P.H., M.S., R.D.
Copy Editor: Diane Rose
Editorial Assistant: Julie Boston
Nutrition Editorial Assistant:
    Rachel Quinlivan, R.D.
Photography Director: Jim Bathie
Senior Photo Stylist: Kay E. Clarke
Photo Stylist: Katherine Eckert
Director, Test Kitchens: Elizabeth Tyler Austin
Assistant Director, Test Kitchens:
    Julie Christopher
Food Stylist: Kelley Self Wilton
Test Kitchens Staff: Kathleen Royal Phillips,
    Catherine Crowell Steele, Ashley T. Strickland
Director of Production: Laura Lockhart
Production Manager: Terri Beste
Production Assistant: Faye Porter Bonner

Contributors:
Designer: Carol Damsky
Copy Editor: Dolores Hydock
Indexer: Mary Ann Laurens
Editorial Assistant: Laura K. Womble
Editorial Interns: Jill Baughman, Amy Edgerton,
    Amelia Heying
Photo Stylist: Melanie J. Clarke
Food Stylists: Ana Price Kelly,
    Debby Maugans Nakos
Test Kitchens Staff: Jane Chambliss,
    Kate M. Wheeler, R.D.
Photographers: Mark Gooch, Beau Gustafson

To order additional publications, call
1-800-765-6400, or visit oxmoorhouse.com

CONTENTS

Essential Salads 8

There's nothing quite like a salad to showcase fabulous fresh ingredients. Here, you'll find all of your favorites, including classic Caesar salad, zesty coleslaw, potato salad, and Cobb salad.

For Starters 32

Excite your appetite with a bed of beautiful greens, fresh produce, and dazzling dressings. No matter what you serve as the main course, these recipes will begin your meal in the best of taste.

Entrée Salads 52

If you're craving a light lunch or dinner, turn to these satisfying main dishes. From family-pleasing taco salad to elegant salmon over greens to exotic Thai beef salad, there's a choice here for everyone.

Grain & Pasta Salads 74

Fiber-filled, wholesome grains and delicious pastas make great salads that are filling, almost always portable, and easy to make ahead. Turn here to find a lunch to go or a smart side for a picnic or barbecue.

Vegetable Salads 94

Refreshing vegetable salads highlight the season's best produce like no other dish. From asparagus to spaghetti squash, you'll savor every healthful, colorful, delicious bite.

Fruit Salads 114

Choose one of these sweet, juicy mélanges for a brunch side, a snack, or even a healthy dessert. From a traditional tropical fruit salad to offerings made from strawberries, kiwifruit, stone fruit, and fresh figs, these recipes round out a meal with flair.

Cooking Light®
Editor in Chief: Mary Kay Culpepper
Executive Editor: Billy R. Sims
Art Director: Susan Waldrip Dendy
Managing Editor: Maelynn Cheung
Senior Food Editor: Alison Mann Ashton
Features Editor: Phillip Rhodes
Projects Editor: Mary Simpson Creel, M.S., R.D.
Food Editor: Ann Taylor Pittman
Associate Food Editors: Julianna Grimes Bottcher,
    Timothy Q. Cebula
Assistant Food Editor: Kathy Kitchens Downie, R.D.
Assistant Editors: Cindy Hatcher,
    Brandy Rushing
Test Kitchens Director: Vanessa Taylor Johnson
Senior Food Stylist: Kellie Gerber Kelley
Food Stylist: M. Kathleen Kanen
Test Kitchens Professionals: SaBrina Bone,
    Kathryn Conrad, Mary H. Drennen,
    Jan Jacks Moon, Tiffany Vickers,
    Mike Wilson
Assistant Art Director: Maya Metz Logue
Senior Designers: Fernande Bondarenko,
    J. Shay McNamee
Designer: Brigette Mayer
Senior Photographer: Randy Mayor
Senior Photo Stylist: Cindy Barr
Photo Stylists: Jan Gautro, Leigh Ann Ross
Studio Assistant: Melissa Hoover
Copy Chief: Maria Parker Hopkins
Senior Copy Editor: Susan Roberts
Copy Editor: Johannah Paiva
Production Manager: Liz Rhoades
Production Editors: Joanne McCrary Brasseal,
    Hazel R. Eddins
Administrative Coordinator: Carol D. Johnson
Office Manager: Rita K. Jackson
Editorial Assistant: Abigail Banks
Correspondence Editor: Michelle Gibson Daniels
Intern: Lauri Short

CookingLight.com
Editor: Jennifer Middleton Richards
Online Producer: Abigail Masters

Cover: *Autumn Apple and Spinach Salad (page 42)*

Welcome

Salad is healthful, beautiful, and just plain refreshing. But there's another thing that salad is, and that's essential. For a *Cooking Light*® cook, salad is one of the most delicious items on the table.

In this cookbook, you'll find the salad recipes we at *Cooking Light* believe to be the essential recipes for every *Cooking Light* cook. These recipes are our tried-and-true classics—ones we love to make again and again.

Each chapter offers mouthwatering, flavorful Test Kitchens–approved recipes, complete with our signature nutritional analyses. After all, eating smart, being fit, and living well are essential in our minds.

So whether you're looking for a down-home recipe for Classic Potato Salad or for something a little more refined, such as Frisée, Baby Spinach, and Golden Beet Salad, you're sure to find it in this edition of *The Cooking Light Cook's Essential Recipe Collection*. We hope these recipes will become as essential to your family as they are to the *Cooking Light* family.

Very truly yours,

Mary Kay Culpepper
Editor in Chief

essential
salads

Simple Green Salad with Basic Vinaigrette

6 cups torn curly leaf lettuce
¼ cup thinly vertically sliced
   red onion
1 pint cherry tomatoes, halved
Basic Vinaigrette

1. Place lettuce, sliced onion, and tomatoes in a large bowl; toss gently to combine. Drizzle Basic Vinaigrette over salad; toss gently to coat. Yield: 4 servings (serving size: 2 cups).

(Totals include Basic Vinaigrette) CALORIES 49 (44% from fat); FAT 2.4g (sat 0.3g, mono 1.7g, poly 0.3g); PROTEIN 1.5g; CARB 7.2g; FIBER 2.7g; CHOL 0mg; IRON 0.3mg; SODIUM 189mg; CALC 46mg

Oil and vinegar do not combine naturally, but whisking helps to disperse and suspend tiny droplets of oil in the vinegar. Dijon mustard acts as a binding agent that keeps the mixture from separating. Inexpensive red wine vinegar and olive oil will work fine in this vinaigrette. If you'd like to upgrade, use a premium extravirgin olive oil and a high-quality red wine vinegar, such as an aged vinegar made from the cabernet sauvignon grape, an Italian Chianti or Barolo vinegar, or a Spanish Rioja vinegar.

Basic Vinaigrette

2 tablespoons minced red
   onion
1½ tablespoons red wine
   vinegar
2 teaspoons olive oil
¼ teaspoon salt
¼ teaspoon freshly ground
   black pepper
¼ teaspoon Dijon mustard

1. Combine minced onion and vinegar in a small bowl; let stand 5 minutes. Add olive oil and remaining ingredients; stir well with a whisk. Yield: 3 tablespoons (serving size: 1 tablespoon).

CALORIES 30 (90% from fat); FAT 3g (sat 0.4g, mono 2.2g, poly 0.3g); PROTEIN 0.1g; CARB 0.8g; FIBER 0.1g; CHOL 0mg; IRON 0.1mg; SODIUM 200mg; CALC 3mg

Dress up this basic salad with additional toppings, such as fresh parsley, fresh basil, and a sprinkling of freshly grated Parmesan cheese. Or, to dress it down, simply toss the dressing with field greens.

Creamy Caesar Salad with Spicy Croutons

2 teaspoons olive oil
¾ teaspoon Cajun seasoning
1 garlic clove, minced
2 cups (¾-inch) cubed
   sourdough bread
18 cups torn romaine lettuce
Creamy Caesar Dressing
⅓ cup (1½ ounces) shredded
   fresh Parmesan cheese

1. Preheat oven to 400°.
2. Combine oil, Cajun seasoning, and minced garlic in a medium microwave-safe bowl. Microwave at HIGH 20 seconds. Add bread cubes; toss gently to coat. Spread bread cubes in a single layer on a baking sheet; bake at 400° for 15 minutes.
3. Place lettuce in a large bowl. Add Creamy Caesar Dressing; toss gently to coat. Sprinkle with cheese, and top with croutons. Yield: 6 servings (serving size: 2 cups).

(Totals include Creamy Caesar Dressing) CALORIES 137 (27% from fat); FAT 4.1g (sat 1.3g, mono 1.6g, poly 0.4g); PROTEIN 7.7g; CARB 18.2g; FIBER 4.1g; CHOL 4mg; IRON 3mg; SODIUM 836mg; CALC 176mg

Romaine is the lettuce of choice for a traditional Caesar salad. The leaves grow in heads, ranging from dark green outer leaves to yellowish green leaves at the heart. Baby romaine leaves, which are available pre-washed in packages, offer the same pleasing, slightly bitter flavor of regular romaine. However, for the signature crunch that comes from a romaine leaf's succulent center vein, stick with the full-sized version.

Creamy Caesar Dressing

1 garlic clove, halved
½ cup fat-free mayonnaise
2 tablespoons red wine
   vinegar
2 teaspoons Dijon mustard
2 teaspoons white wine
   Worcestershire sauce
1 teaspoon anchovy paste
¼ teaspoon black pepper

1. Drop garlic halves through opening in blender lid with blender on; process until minced. Add mayonnaise and remaining ingredients; process until well blended. Cover and chill at least 1 hour. Yield: about ½ cup (serving size: 1 tablespoon).

CALORIES 14 (32% from fat); FAT 0.5g (sat 0.1g, mono 0g, poly 0g); PROTEIN 0.2g; CARB 2.5g; FIBER 0.4g; CHOL 2mg; IRON 0.2mg; SODIUM 252mg; CALC 7mg

Creamy dressing, crunchy croutons, and a characteristic Mediterranean bite make Caesar salad hard to turn down. Our lightened version has all the zing of the original: Garlic, anchovies, and Parmesan cheese drive its taste. But we've dismissed the egg yolks and heavy oil and turned to fat-free mayonnaise to form the base of the dressing and still give a mouthful of flavor. We've added a Cajun kick, too, with lightly spiced croutons.

Iceberg Wedge with Pancetta

Cooking spray
  1 ounce pancetta, diced
    (about 3 tablespoons)
  1 head iceberg lettuce
  ½ cup Chive-Buttermilk
    Dressing
  1 cup chopped tomato
  ½ cup diced English cucumber

1. Heat a nonstick skillet over medium-high heat; coat pan with cooking spray. Add pancetta to pan; cook 3 minutes or until crisp. Drain on paper towels.

2. Cut lettuce head in half; cut each half into 2 wedges. Place wedges on 4 salad plates. Drizzle with Chive-Buttermilk Dressing; top with tomato and cucumber. Sprinkle evenly with pancetta. Yield: 4 servings (serving size: 1 lettuce wedge, 2 tablespoons dressing, ¼ cup tomato, 2 tablespoons cucumber, and about 2 teaspoons pancetta).

(Totals include Chive-Buttermilk Dressing) CALORIES 80 (44% from fat); FAT 3.9g (sat 1.4g, mono 0g, poly 0.2g); PROTEIN 3.6g; CARB 9g; FIBER 2.3g; CHOL 5mg; IRON 0.7mg; SODIUM 331mg; CALC 60mg

This all-purpose dressing's ranchlike flavor and texture will be a hit at your dinner table. You'll have extra dressing left over after making this salad, but it will keep in the refrigerator in an airtight container for up to five days (stir well before using). Use the leftovers as a marinade for chicken, as a dressing for another salad, or as a dip for cut-up vegetables.

Chive-Buttermilk Dressing

  ¾ cup fat-free buttermilk
  ⅓ cup light mayonnaise
  2 to 3 teaspoons finely
    chopped fresh chives
  1 teaspoon finely chopped
    fresh basil
  2 teaspoons Dijon mustard
  ½ teaspoon coarsely ground
    black pepper
  ¼ teaspoon salt
  1 garlic clove, minced

1. Combine all ingredients, stirring with a whisk until well blended. Yield: 1 cup (serving size: 1 tablespoon).

CALORIES 13 (48% from fat); FAT 0.7g (sat 0.2g, mono 0g, poly 0g); PROTEIN 0.5g; CARB 1.4g; FIBER 0g; CHOL 0mg; IRON 0mg; SODIUM 99mg; CALC 15mg

Pancetta—Italian bacon that has been cured but not smoked—updates this classic salad. You can use regular bacon in its place. Serve with a fork and knife to cut up the iceberg wedge.

Three-Pepper Slaw

½ cup thinly sliced red bell
    pepper strips
½ cup thinly sliced green bell
    pepper strips
⅓ cup chopped green onions
¼ cup finely chopped seeded
    jalapeño pepper
1 (10-ounce) package angel
    hair coleslaw (about 6 cups)
¼ cup white wine vinegar
2 tablespoons fresh lime juice
1 teaspoon sugar
2 teaspoons canola oil
½ teaspoon salt
¼ teaspoon white pepper

1. Place first 5 ingredients in a large bowl, tossing to combine.

2. Combine vinegar and next 5 ingredients in a small bowl, stirring with a whisk. Pour vinegar mixture over coleslaw mixture, tossing to coat. Yield: 8 servings (serving size: about ¾ cup).

CALORIES 29 (39% from fat); FAT 1.3g (sat 0.1g, mono 0.7g, poly 0.4g); PROTEIN 0.8g; CARB 4.5g; FIBER 0.2g; CHOL 0mg; IRON 0.3mg; SODIUM 153mg; CALC 21mg

White pepper is ground white peppercorns, which are the mature, hulled berries of the *Piper nigrum* vine. (Black and green peppercorns, on the other hand, are picked while still immature.) White pepper has a pungent flavor but is milder than black pepper. Whole white peppercorns are often used in marinades and as a pickling spice. Ground white pepper is useful for seasoning light-colored foods, such as mashed potatoes or this slaw, without discoloring them.

For convenience, we used packaged angel hair coleslaw. If you prefer, use a very sharp chef's knife or mandoline to cut a head of cabbage into very thin strips. The sliced cabbage will resemble angel hair pasta, which explains the coleslaw's name. This quick and easy crunchy slaw goes well with grilled meats and Tex-Mex dishes.

Mozzarella-Tomato Salad

1 medium red tomato, cut into
  6 slices
1 medium yellow tomato, cut
  into 6 slices
8 ounces fresh mozzarella
  cheese, cut into 12 slices
¾ cup fresh basil leaves
4 teaspoons extravirgin olive
  oil
½ teaspoon salt
½ teaspoon freshly ground
  black pepper

1. Layer tomato slices alternately with cheese slices on 4 salad plates; top evenly with basil leaves. Drizzle with oil, and sprinkle each with ⅛ teaspoon salt and ⅛ teaspoon pepper. Serve immediately. Yield: 4 servings (serving size: 3 tomato slices, 3 cheese slices, 3 tablespoons basil, and 1 teaspoon oil).

CALORIES 222 (70% from fat); FAT 17.1g (sat 8.8g, mono 3.6g, poly 0.5g); PROTEIN 10.9g; CARB 5.2g; FIBER 1.1g; CHOL 45mg; IRON 0.9mg; SODIUM 379mg; CALC 337mg

Ground black pepper packaged in a tin or a jar is convenient, but it lacks the natural oil that helps give the spice its bite. Grinding fresh whole peppercorns just before you need them releases their oils, resulting in a more vivid flavor that's key for a simple salad like this. In our experience, 10 full cranks of a pepper mill produces about ¼ teaspoon of coarsely ground pepper.

This traditional Italian salad is also known as insalata Caprese, meaning "salad in the style of Capri," an island in the region of Campania. Top-quality fresh ingredients are the key to this salad's success. Use heirloom tomatoes if they're available.

Cobb Salad with Green Goddess Dressing

Watercress, a member of the mustard family, is one of the traditional ingredients of a Cobb salad. It grows wild in cool running streams and brooks and has small, crisp dark green leaves with a sharp, peppery flavor. This green is sold year-round in small bunches in the super-market. When buying it, look for leaves with a deep green color. If you cannot find watercress, another pungent-flavored green, such as arugula, makes a good substitute.

8 cups torn romaine lettuce
1 cup trimmed watercress
1½ cups chopped cooked chicken breast
2 tomatoes, each cut into 8 wedges (about 1 pound)
2 hard-cooked large eggs, each cut into 4 wedges
½ cup diced peeled avocado
¼ cup plus 2 tablespoons (1½ ounces) crumbled blue cheese
Green Goddess Dressing

1. Combine lettuce and watercress in a large bowl. Divide lettuce mixture among 4 plates. Arrange chicken, tomato wedges, egg wedges, avocado, and cheese over lettuce mixture. Serve with Green Goddess Dressing. Yield: 4 servings (serving size: about 2 cups lettuce mixture, 6 tablespoons chicken, 4 tomato wedges, 2 egg wedges, 2 tablespoons avocado, 1½ tablespoons cheese, and ¼ cup dressing).

CALORIES 301 (47% from fat); FAT 15.7g (sat 4.8g, mono 3.5g, poly 1.3g); PROTEIN 26g; CARB 14.4g; FIBER 3.7g; CHOL 167mg; IRON 3.2mg; SODIUM 670mg; CALC 196mg

Green Goddess Dressing

½ cup plain fat-free yogurt
¼ cup light mayonnaise
3 tablespoons chopped green onions
3 tablespoons white wine vinegar
2 tablespoons chopped fresh flat-leaf parsley
1 tablespoon chopped fresh chives
2 teaspoons anchovy paste
1 teaspoon chopped fresh tarragon
¼ teaspoon freshly ground black pepper
⅛ teaspoon salt
1 garlic clove, minced

1. Place all ingredients in a blender or food processor; process until smooth. Chill. Yield: 1 cup (serving size: 1 tablespoon).

CALORIES 18 (65% from fat); FAT 1.3g (sat 0.3g, mono 0g, poly 0g); PROTEIN 0.4g; CARB 1.2g; FIBER 0.1g; CHOL 2mg; IRON 0.3mg; SODIUM 109mg; CALC 14mg

In this healthy version of Cobb salad, we've foregone the usual bacon and decreased the amount of cheese. You won't miss these high-fat ingredients when you top this salad with our creamy, flavor-packed Green Goddess Dressing, which is named for its signature green tint.

Chicken Salad

1¾ cups chopped cooked
  chicken breast
⅓ cup diced celery
¼ cup finely chopped green
  onions
¼ cup light mayonnaise
3 tablespoons chopped fresh
  parsley
2 tablespoons plain fat-free
  yogurt
1 tablespoon lemon juice
½ teaspoon salt
½ teaspoon dried basil
¼ teaspoon black pepper
1 (2-ounce) jar diced pimiento,
  drained

1. Combine all ingredients in a bowl; stir well. Cover and chill up to 2 days. Yield: 4 servings (serving size: ½ cup).

CALORIES 168 (42% from fat); FAT 7.8g (sat 1.8g, mono 1g, poly 0.6g); PROTEIN 19.6g; CARB 3.6g; FIBER 0.8g; CHOL 57mg; IRON 1.1mg; SODIUM 476mg; CALC 36mg

The pimiento, whose name is the Spanish word for "pepper," is a large heart-shaped pepper that's more flavorful than the red bell pepper. Pimientos are most easily found canned or jarred in whole, sliced, and diced varieties. They're a mainstay in stuffed olives, pimiento cheese, and casseroles. The pimiento's sweet flavor is a nice complement to the herbs and crunchy celery in this tasty chicken salad.

Surround a scoop of our herbed chicken salad with crisp crackers and a variety of seasonal fruit for a light lunch or dinner.

Macaroni Salad

Cool the cooked macaroni completely before tossing the salad so that the cheese doesn't melt. A quick way to do this is to rinse the pasta in a colander under cool running water and then drain it well. This washes away some of the starch, making the pasta less sticky. Though this starch is useful for helping sauces adhere to pasta in warm dishes, chilled pasta salads benefit from having less starch.

3 cups cooked medium elbow macaroni (about 1½ cups uncooked)
¾ cup (3 ounces) reduced-fat shredded sharp Cheddar cheese
½ cup frozen green peas, thawed
½ cup diced lean ham
¼ cup sliced green onions
1 cup light mayonnaise
½ teaspoon salt
¼ teaspoon black pepper

1. Combine first 5 ingredients in a bowl, and toss well. Combine mayonnaise, salt, and pepper; stir well. Add mayonnaise mixture to salad, and toss well. Cover and chill. Yield: 8 servings (serving size: ⅔ cup).

CALORIES 232 (53% from fat); FAT 13.6g (sat 4g, mono 0.4g, poly 0.2g); PROTEIN 8.3g; CARB 18.8g; FIBER 1.3g; CHOL 26mg; IRON 1mg; SODIUM 399mg; CALC 90mg

This classic make-ahead salad is perfect for a lunch buffet or a picnic. Always keep any salad with a mayonnaise-based dressing cold for food safety.

Mixed Bean Salad with Sun-Dried Tomatoes

1 (8-ounce) jar oil-packed
  sun-dried tomato halves
½ cup chopped fresh parsley
½ cup chopped fresh basil
1 (15.8-ounce) can black-eyed
  peas, rinsed and drained
1 (15-ounce) can red kidney
  beans, rinsed and drained
1 (15-ounce) can white kidney
  beans, rinsed and drained
1 (15-ounce) can black beans,
  rinsed and drained
½ red onion, thinly sliced
⅓ cup red wine vinegar
¼ cup sugar
½ teaspoon salt
½ teaspoon dry mustard
¼ teaspoon freshly ground
  black pepper

1. Drain tomato halves in a sieve over a bowl, reserving oil. Place ¼ cup oil in a medium bowl. Return remaining oil to jar; refrigerate and reserve for another use.
2. Chop drained tomatoes; place in a large bowl. Add parsley and next 6 ingredients, and stir gently to combine.
3. Add vinegar and next 4 ingredients to ¼ cup reserved oil, stirring with a whisk. Drizzle over bean mixture; toss gently to coat. Cover and chill. Yield: 14 servings (serving size: ½ cup).

CALORIES 181 (28% from fat); FAT 5.7g (sat 0.7g, mono 3.6g, poly 0.9g); PROTEIN 7.2g; CARB 26.2g; FIBER 4.4g; CHOL 0mg; IRON 2.5mg; SODIUM 417mg; CALC 100mg

The jar of oil-packed sun-dried tomatoes in this recipe does double duty. The dried tomatoes provide an intensely sweet tang that contrasts with the mellow beans, and the oil from the jar is used as a base for the dressing. Be sure to save the leftover oil, which takes on a golden orange color from the toma-toes. You can use it in another dressing or as a flavored dip-ping oil for bread.

Here's a great choice for your next potluck party. You can make it ahead; it tastes even better after the flavors have had time to meld. Rinsing and draining the beans and peas improves the appearance of the salad and reduces the sodium content.

Classic Potato Salad

1½ pounds baking potatoes,
    halved
½ cup finely chopped red
    onion
¼ cup finely chopped celery
¼ cup sweet pickle relish
2 hard-cooked large eggs,
    coarsely chopped
⅓ cup light mayonnaise
2 tablespoons cider vinegar
1 tablespoon Dijon mustard
¼ teaspoon salt
¼ teaspoon black pepper

1. Cook potatoes in boiling water 25 minutes or until tender; drain and cool completely.

2. Cut potatoes into ½-inch cubes. Combine potato, onion, and next 3 ingredients in a large bowl. Combine mayonnaise and next 4 ingredients in a small bowl; stir with a whisk. Pour mayonnaise mixture over potato mixture, tossing gently to coat. Cover and chill at least 8 hours. Yield: 6 servings (serving size: ¾ cup).

CALORIES 208 (25% from fat); FAT 5.7g (sat 1.1g, mono 1.7g, poly 2.2g); PROTEIN 5g; CARB 35.1g; FIBER 2.4g; CHOL 75mg; IRON 1.9mg; SODIUM 387mg; CALC 26mg

Sweet pickle relish is an essential ingredient of traditional potato salad, egg salad, and tuna salad. It's usually made from cucumbers and bell peppers pickled in a mixture of vinegar, corn syrup or sugar, and, on occasion, spices. The sweet-and-sour combination adds zing wherever it's used.

There are no surprises here—just good old-fashioned comfort food. We left the skins on the potatoes for extra fiber, but you can peel them if you choose. Serve this alongside ham for Easter or with burgers for the Fourth of July. And, of course, it will be welcome on the table any other time of year, too.

Fruited Port-Cranberry Salad

1 envelope unflavored gelatin
½ cup port or other sweet red wine
2 (3-ounce) packages cranberry-flavored gelatin
¼ teaspoon ground ginger
¼ teaspoon ground allspice
2 cups boiling water
1 (16-ounce) can whole-berry cranberry sauce
½ cup ice water
1½ cups finely chopped Granny Smith apple (about 1 large)
1 (14-ounce) package frozen unsweetened raspberries, thawed
1 (8-ounce) can crushed pineapple in juice, drained

1. Sprinkle unflavored gelatin over port; let stand 1 minute.

2. Combine cranberry-flavored gelatin, ginger, and allspice in a large bowl; stir well. Add boiling water and port mixture, stirring until gelatin dissolves. Add cranberry sauce and ice water; stir well. Chill 30 minutes.

3. Combine apple, raspberries, and pineapple; stir into gelatin mixture. Pour into an 8-cup gelatin mold; chill 4 hours or until set. To unmold, dip mold into hot water 5 seconds; invert onto a serving platter. Yield: 12 servings (serving size: 1 slice).

CALORIES 178 (1% from fat); FAT 0.2g (sat 0g, mono 0g, poly 0.1g); PROTEIN 2.3g; CARB 41.3g; FIBER 2g; CHOL 0mg; IRON 0.4mg; SODIUM 63mg; CALC 10mg

Gelatin is what makes a molded salad keep its shape. This recipe uses both unflavored and sweetened flavored gelatin, and the two different types must be handled differently. The unflavored type must first soften in a cold liquid for 1 to 5 minutes, which is why we sprinkled it over the port before combining it with the other ingredients. You can skip that step with flavored gelatin, but both types must be dissolved completely in the boiling water before the ice water is added.

This is not your ordinary congealed salad. It gets its deep red color from the cranberry sauce, raspberries, and cranberry-flavored gelatin; its tartness and crunch from the chopped apple; and its rich, slightly sweet flavor from the port. It's perfect for a holiday buffet when served on a platter lined with leaf lettuce.

for starters

Arugula, White Bean, and Roasted Red Pepper Salad

Salad:
- 3 cups arugula leaves
- ½ cup chopped bottled roasted red bell peppers
- ⅓ cup vertically sliced red onion
- 1 (16-ounce) can navy beans, rinsed and drained

Dressing:
- 1½ tablespoons balsamic vinegar
- 1 tablespoon olive oil
- 1 teaspoon honey
- ¼ teaspoon salt
- ¼ teaspoon black pepper
- 1 garlic clove, minced

1. To prepare salad, combine first 4 ingredients in a large serving bowl.

2. To prepare dressing, combine vinegar and next 5 ingredients in a small bowl, stirring with a whisk until blended. Pour over salad, and toss to coat. Yield: 4 servings (serving size: 1 cup).

CALORIES 164 (29% from fat); FAT 5.3g (sat 0.7g, mono 2.9g, poly 1.2g); PROTEIN 7.1g; CARB 23.6g; FIBER 2.9g; CHOL 0mg; IRON 2.3mg; SODIUM 500mg; CALC 80mg

Balsamic vinegar has a pungent sweetness that adds a pleasant tang to vinaigrettes. Prices for balsamic vinegar vary greatly depending on the quality, but we recommend a middle-of-the-road variety for everyday use, such as Alessi's four-year balsamic vinegar. See page 139 for more information on balsamic vinegar.

Sweet roasted red bell peppers and nutty beans are convenient additions that round out the flavors of peppery arugula and crisp red onions. Since this salad doesn't take much preparation, it's a good choice when you want an elegant first course but are short on time. Baby spinach has a milder flavor than arugula and is a good substitute for it.

Jícama-Avocado Salad with Pomegranate-Lime Dressing

2 tablespoons fresh lime juice
2 tablespoons fresh
   pomegranate juice
1 teaspoon sugar
¾ teaspoon salt
¼ teaspoon ground cumin
1 small garlic clove, minced
1 teaspoon olive oil
2 cups arugula leaves
1½ cups (3-inch) julienne-cut
   peeled jícama
½ cup vertically sliced red
   onion
½ cup diced peeled avocado
2 tablespoons chopped fresh
   cilantro
¼ cup fresh pomegranate
   seeds
4 teaspoons pine nuts, toasted

1. Combine first 6 ingredients in a large bowl. Add oil, and stir with a whisk. Add arugula and next 4 ingredients, and toss gently. Divide salad among 4 salad plates. Top with pomegranate seeds and pine nuts. Serve immediately. Yield: 4 servings (serving size: 1 cup salad, 1 tablespoon pomegranate seeds, and 1 teaspoon pine nuts).

CALORIES 126 (44% from fat); FAT 6.1g (sat 0.8g, mono 3.1g, poly 1.5g); PROTEIN 1.8g; CARB 18.7g; FIBER 4g; CHOL 0mg; IRON 1mg; SODIUM 444mg; CALC 32mg

The pomegranate is one of the oldest cultivated fruits, but we are just beginning to understand its benefits. It's an excellent source of polyphenols (the same healthful compounds found in red wine and green tea), vitamin C, potassium, and calcium. Studies suggest that the fruit may keep fatty deposits from forming on artery walls and may prevent prostate cancer. For this recipe, cut a small pomegranate in half; remove the seeds from one half, and squeeze the juice from the other. Wear gloves and an old shirt or an apron to protect your hands and clothes from stains.

Both the sweet-tart pomegranate seeds and the dressing brighten the mild jícama and the buttery avocados and pine nuts. The jícama also contributes a nice crunch.

Escarole Salad with Melons and Crispy Prosciutto

Escarole is a variety of endive but is not as bitter as Belgian endive or curly endive. It has broad bright green leaves that grow in loose heads. When purchasing escarole, look for fresh, crisp leaves without discoloration. Store escarole tightly wrapped in the refrigerator for up to three days.

4 thin slices prosciutto (about 1.5 ounces), coarsely chopped
3 tablespoons minced shallots
2 tablespoons balsamic vinegar
1 tablespoon red wine vinegar
1½ teaspoons extravirgin olive oil
¼ teaspoon salt
¼ teaspoon freshly ground black pepper
12 cups torn escarole (about 1¼ pounds)
2 cups torn radicchio (about 4 ounces)
2 cups cubed peeled honeydew melon
2 cups cubed peeled cantaloupe
2 tablespoons sliced almonds, toasted

1. Preheat oven to 400°.
2. Arrange prosciutto in a single layer on a baking sheet. Bake at 400° for 6 minutes or until crisp.
3. Combine shallots and next 5 ingredients in a large bowl, stirring with a whisk. Add escarole and radicchio, and toss to coat. Add honeydew and cantaloupe, and toss to combine. Divide salad among 6 salad plates, and sprinkle with prosciutto and almonds. Yield: 6 servings (serving size: 2 cups salad, about 2 teaspoons prosciutto, and 1 teaspoon almonds).

CALORIES 105 (32% from fat); FAT 3.7g (sat 0.7g, mono 2.1g, poly 0.6g); PROTEIN 3.6g; CARB 16.4g; FIBER 4g; CHOL 4mg; IRON 1.1mg; SODIUM 228mg; CALC 68mg

If you're looking for a salad to whet the appetite, then this is it. The crispy bits of salty prosciutto pair well with the bitterness of the escarole and radicchio. The subtle, sweet flavors of the honeydew and cantaloupe are enhanced by a splash each of balsamic and red wine vinegar. This refreshing salad is an ideal companion for grilled meat.

Frisée, Baby Spinach, and Golden Beet Salad

Frisée, a member of the chicory family, has a slightly bitter yet pleasing taste. Its pale yellow-green leaves are narrow and curly and have a frizzy appearance. Because of its unique form, frisée creates texture and variation on a plate of two-dimensional salad greens. Frisée holds up nicely to the weight of salad dressing, while its counterparts succumb and become soggy if dressed for too long.

¾ pound golden beets
1 cup cranberry juice cocktail
⅓ cup sweetened dried cranberries
3 tablespoons sugar
2 tablespoons raspberry vinegar
1 tablespoon minced shallots
¼ teaspoon salt
¼ teaspoon freshly ground black pepper
1 tablespoon walnut oil
4 cups frisée or radicchio
4 cups baby spinach
½ cup (2 ounces) crumbled soft (log-style) goat cheese

1. Preheat oven to 400°.
2. Wrap each beet in foil. Bake at 400° for 1½ hours or until tender. Discard foil; cool beets 30 minutes. Trim off roots, and rub off skins. Cut beets into ⅛-inch-thick slices.
3. Combine cranberry juice, cranberries, sugar, and vinegar in a small saucepan. Bring to a boil; cook 11 minutes or until thick. Remove from heat. Stir in shallots, salt, and pepper. Gradually add oil, stirring with a whisk.
4. Combine frisée and spinach in a large bowl. Add cranberry mixture, and toss to coat. Add beets; toss gently to combine. Divide salad evenly among 6 salad plates. Top with cheese. Yield: 6 servings (serving size: about 1½ cups salad and 4 teaspoons cheese).

CALORIES 175 (28% from fat); FAT 5.4g (sat 2.2g, mono 1.2g, poly 1.6g); PROTEIN 4.2g; CARB 28.7g; FIBER 3.3g; CHOL 7mg; IRON 1.7mg; SODIUM 214mg; CALC 74mg

Goat cheese and cranberries bring a bit of tartness to the mellow sweetness of roasted beets. Raspberry vinegar and walnut oil are not common pantry items, but the flavor they bring to the dressing makes them well worth buying.

Autumn Apple and Spinach Salad

The distinctively robust and sharp flavor of blue cheese drives people to love it or hate it. Its most distinguishing feature is its white interior, which is streaked with bluish veins. The texture can vary from crumbly to creamy. Some of the world's oldest and most famous cheeses—Stilton, Gorgonzola, and Roquefort—are blues. Whether its source is goat's, cow's, or sheep's milk, a little blue packs a potent punch. Blue cheese pairs well with fruits, such as apples, pears, and strawberries, which balance and accentuate its flavor.

2 tablespoons fresh orange juice
2 tablespoons fresh lime juice
2 teaspoons Dijon mustard
2 teaspoons honey
¼ teaspoon salt
⅛ teaspoon freshly ground black pepper
8 cups bagged prewashed baby spinach (about 8 ounces)
½ cup thinly vertically sliced red onion
1 large firm sweet-tart apple, cored and thinly sliced
¼ cup (1 ounce) crumbled blue cheese

1. Combine first 6 ingredients, stirring well with a whisk.
2. Combine spinach, onion, and apple in a large bowl. Drizzle with dressing; toss gently to coat. Sprinkle with cheese. Yield: 6 servings (serving size: about 1⅓ cups).

CALORIES 60 (29% from fat); FAT 1.9g (sat 1g, mono 0.5g, poly 0.1g); PROTEIN 2.7g; CARB 9.4g; FIBER 2.2g; CHOL 4mg; IRON 1.3mg; SODIUM 251mg; CALC 76mg

Crisp sweet-tart apples are an ideal complement to the intense flavor and creamy texture of blue cheese. Try Goldrush or Braeburn apples, which both have a nice balance of sweetness and acidity.

(pictured on cover)

Watercress Salad with Blue Cheese and Praline

Watch the praline mixture carefully as it cooks. The sugar should cook until it's golden, but it can quickly burn if cooked longer. The caramelized sugar hardens as it cools, resulting in a product similar to a brittle. You can make the praline pieces a couple of days ahead, but be warned: These candy-like treats are a tempting snack by themselves!

Dressing:
  1 tablespoon water
  1½ teaspoons fresh lemon juice
  1 teaspoon Dijon mustard
  ½ teaspoon extravirgin olive oil
  ⅛ teaspoon black pepper
Dash of salt
Dash of dried tarragon
  1 small garlic clove, minced
Praline:
  ¼ cup sugar
  2 tablespoons chopped
    walnuts
Cooking spray
Salad:
  1 cup trimmed watercress
  1 cup Boston lettuce leaves
  1 tablespoon crumbled blue
    cheese or feta cheese

1. To prepare dressing, combine first 8 ingredients; stir well with a whisk.

2. To prepare praline, place sugar in a small skillet over medium heat, and cook until sugar dissolves, stirring to dissolve sugar evenly. Stir in chopped walnuts, and cook over low heat 30 seconds or until golden. Remove from heat. Rapidly spread mixture onto foil coated with cooking spray. Cool completely; break into small pieces.

3. To prepare salad, combine watercress, lettuce, and blue cheese in a bowl; add dressing and praline, tossing well. Yield: 2 servings (serving size: 1½ cups).

CALORIES 180 (34% from fat); FAT 6.8g (sat 1.1g, mono 2.1g, poly 3.1g); PROTEIN 3.6g; CARB 28g; FIBER 1.4g; CHOL 3mg; IRON 0.7mg; SODIUM 280mg; CALC 58mg

A dash of tarragon imparts a delicate licorice flavor to the light lemony dressing. Peppery watercress and buttery-textured Boston lettuce make a fitting bed for the pungent cheese and sweet praline pieces.

Mixed Greens with Roasted Tomato and Goat Cheese

This sweet, tangy dressing can pull double-duty as a marinade for rich meats, such as pork or dark-meat chicken. Be sure to use real maple syrup and not maple-flavored corn syrup. Pure maple syrup has a clean, distinct flavor and a subtle bouquet that can't be reproduced. Another key component of this dressing is the tomato juice, which helps marry the dressing with the roasted tomatoes in this salad.

1 cup grape or cherry
    tomatoes, halved
¼ cup Maple-Balsamic
    Dressing, divided
Cooking spray
8 cups loosely packed baby
    arugula, watercress, or
    spinach (about 4 ounces)
¼ cup thinly vertically sliced
    red onion
2 tablespoons crumbled goat
    cheese
¼ teaspoon freshly ground
    black pepper

1. Preheat oven to 350°.
2. Combine tomatoes and 2 tablespoons Maple-Balsamic Dressing; toss well to coat. Arrange tomatoes, cut sides up, on a jelly-roll pan coated with cooking spray. Bake at 350° for 30 minutes or until tomatoes soften. Cool completely.
3. Combine tomatoes, arugula, and onion in a large bowl. Drizzle with remaining 2 tablespoons Maple-Balsamic Dressing; toss gently to coat. Divide salad among 6 plates. Sprinkle with cheese and pepper. Yield: 6 servings (serving size: about 1⅓ cups salad and 1 teaspoon cheese).

(Totals include Maple-Balsamic Dressing) CALORIES 47 (44% from fat); FAT 2.3g (sat 0.6g, mono 1.3g, poly 0.3g); PROTEIN 1.5g; CARB 6g; FIBER 0.9g; CHOL 1mg; IRON 0.7mg; SODIUM 97mg; CALC 54mg

Maple-Balsamic Dressing

½ cup tomato juice
⅓ cup balsamic vinegar
¼ cup maple syrup
1 tablespoon minced fresh
    rosemary
2 teaspoons Dijon mustard
½ teaspoon salt
½ teaspoon freshly ground
    black pepper
2 garlic cloves, minced
2½ tablespoons extravirgin olive
    oil

1. Combine all ingredients except oil, stirring well. Gradually add oil, stirring constantly with a whisk until mixture is well combined. Yield: about 1 cup (serving size: 1 tablespoon).
Note: Refrigerate dressing in an airtight container for up to 5 days; stir well before using.

CALORIES 39 (53% from fat); FAT 2.3g (sat 0.3g, mono 1.7g, poly 0.2g); PROTEIN 0.2g; CARB 4.7g; FIBER 0.1g; CHOL 0mg; IRON 0.2mg; SODIUM 118mg; CALC 8mg

After roasting, the grape tomatoes will be absolutely bursting with a tart sweetness that's the focal point of this salad. Use your favorite salad greens for this tasty first course. We liked the combination of watercress and arugula, but any other greens will work.

Fennel, Parsley, and Radicchio Salad with Pine Nuts and Raisins

Golden raisins come from the same grape as dark raisins—the Thompson seedless grape—but they're sprayed with sulphur dioxide to prevent darkening and are not dried as long. Raisins add a burst of sweetness to any salad. We plumped them in boiling water for this elegant salad to soften their chewy texture and to brighten their color.

⅓ cup golden raisins
4 cups thinly sliced fennel bulb (about 1 large bulb)
4 cups torn radicchio (about 1 medium head)
1½ cups loosely packed fresh flat-leaf parsley leaves
¼ cup fresh orange juice
1½ tablespoons red wine vinegar
2 teaspoons extravirgin olive oil
½ teaspoon salt
¼ teaspoon freshly ground black pepper
2 tablespoons pine nuts, toasted

1. Place raisins in a small saucepan, and cover with water. Bring to a boil; remove from heat. Cover and let stand 10 minutes. Drain well.
2. Place fennel, radicchio, and parsley in a large bowl, and toss gently to combine. Combine orange juice and next 4 ingredients, stirring well with a whisk. Stir in raisins. Drizzle orange juice mixture over fennel mixture, and toss gently to coat. Divide salad among 6 salad plates, and sprinkle with nuts. Yield: 6 servings (serving size: 1⅓ cups salad and 1 teaspoon nuts).

CALORIES 91 (38% from fat); FAT 3.8g (sat 0.4g, mono 1.7g, poly 1.2g); PROTEIN 2.3g; CARB 14.3g; FIBER 3g; CHOL 0mg; IRON 1.9mg; SODIUM 243mg; CALC 61mg

The bold flavors of licorice-like fennel, clean-tasting parsley, and bitter radicchio achieve a pleasing balance, especially when tossed with the citrusy vinaigrette.

Roasted Squash Salad with Bacon and Pumpkin Seeds

Roasted pumpkin seeds, also known as pepitas, not only have a delicious subtly sweet and nutty flavor but are also some of the most nutritious seeds you can find. In addition to providing heart-healthy fats and protein, they are a very good source of magnesium, manganese, and phosphorous. They're a good source of iron, copper, protein, and zinc, too. For optimal freshness, store the seeds in an airtight container in the refrigerator and use them within two months of the purchase date.

4 cups (½-inch) cubed peeled butternut squash (about 1 pound)
Cooking spray
½ teaspoon salt, divided
½ teaspoon freshly ground black pepper, divided
2 tablespoons sherry vinegar
1 teaspoon Dijon mustard
1 bacon slice
1 shallot, minced
10 cups gourmet salad greens (about 10 ounces)
3 tablespoons unsalted pumpkin-seed kernels, toasted

1. Preheat oven to 400°.

2. Arrange squash in a single layer on a jelly-roll pan coated with cooking spray. Coat squash with cooking spray; sprinkle evenly with ¼ teaspoon salt and ¼ teaspoon pepper. Bake at 400° for 30 minutes or until squash is tender and lightly browned, stirring after 15 minutes. Remove from heat; keep warm.

3. Combine remaining ¼ teaspoon salt, remaining ¼ teaspoon pepper, vinegar, and mustard.

4. Cook bacon in a small nonstick skillet over medium-high heat until crisp. Remove bacon from pan, reserving 1 teaspoon drippings in pan. Crumble bacon; set aside. Add minced shallot to drippings in pan, and sauté 1 minute. Add shallot and bacon to vinegar mixture, stirring with a whisk.

5. Place salad greens in a large serving bowl. Drizzle vinegar mixture over greens; toss gently to coat. Top with squash and pumpkin-seed kernels. Yield: 6 servings (serving size: 1⅓ cups salad, ⅔ cup squash, and 1½ teaspoons kernels).

CALORIES 130 (25% from fat); FAT 3.6g (sat 0.9g, mono 0.9g, poly 1.2g); PROTEIN 4.8g; CARB 23.8g; FIBER 5.5g; CHOL 2mg; IRON 3.2mg; SODIUM 275mg; CALC 134mg

A warm bacon-shallot vinaigrette is a savory complement to sweet roasted squash, while the pumpkin seeds are a crunchy contrast. Serve with pork chops or add grilled chicken.

entrée salads

Taco Rice Salad

When you first open a package of yellow rice, you may be surprised that it doesn't look yellow at all. That's because yellow rice is simply white rice seasoned with brightly colored spices, such as saffron (the dried stamens of the saffron crocus flowers), turmeric (also known as Indian saffron), and safflower (also called saffron thistle). When cooked, these spices give a luminous golden yellow hue to the rice.

Salad:
Cooking spray
1 pound ground round
1 garlic clove, minced
3 cups cooked yellow rice
1 teaspoon ground cumin
1 teaspoon chili powder
¼ teaspoon salt
¼ teaspoon black pepper
6 cups torn romaine lettuce (about 10 ounces)
3 cups chopped tomato (about 1¼ pounds)
1 cup frozen whole-kernel corn, thawed
½ cup chopped red onion
1 (15-ounce) can black beans, rinsed and drained

Dressing:
⅔ cup fat-free sour cream
⅔ cup picante sauce
1 teaspoon chili powder
½ teaspoon ground cumin

Remaining Ingredient:
½ cup (2 ounces) reduced-fat shredded sharp Cheddar cheese

1. To prepare salad, heat a large nonstick skillet over medium-high heat; coat pan with cooking spray. Add beef and garlic, and cook 9 minutes or until browned and done, stirring to crumble. Drain; return beef mixture to pan. Stir in rice and next 4 ingredients. Cool slightly.

2. Place lettuce and next 4 ingredients in a large bowl; toss to combine.

3. To prepare dressing, combine sour cream and next 3 ingredients, stirring with a whisk. Spoon dressing over lettuce mixture; toss to coat. Divide lettuce mixture among 6 plates. Top with rice mixture and cheese. Yield: 6 servings (serving size: 1⅓ cups lettuce mixture, ¾ cup rice mixture, and about 1½ tablespoons cheese).

CALORIES 360 (30% from fat); FAT 11.9g (sat 5g, mono 4.5g, poly 0.8g); PROTEIN 21.1g; CARB 46.7g; FIBER 6.7g; CHOL 48mg; IRON 4.2mg; SODIUM 994mg; CALC 177mg

Packed with classic taco fillings, this easy one-dish meal appeals to kids and adults alike. Convenience products, such as canned beans, frozen corn, preseasoned rice, and commercial picante sauce, make it supereasy to toss together this salad. Serve with light tortilla chips for an added crunch.

Thai Beef Salad

1 (1-pound) flank steak,
    trimmed
Cooking spray
⅓ cup sliced shallots
¼ cup chopped fresh cilantro
3 tablespoons fresh lime juice
1 tablespoon fish sauce
2 teaspoons sliced Thai red
    chiles or serrano chiles
2 medium tomatoes, cut into
    ¼-inch-thick wedges (about
    ¾ pound)

1. Prepare grill or preheat broiler.
2. Place steak on grill rack or broiler pan coated with cooking spray; cook 6 minutes on each side or until desired degree of doneness. Place on a cutting board; cover loosely with foil. Let steak stand 10 minutes. Cut steak diagonally across grain into thin slices; cut each slice into 2-inch pieces.
3. Combine steak, shallots, and remaining ingredients, and toss gently. Yield: 4 servings (serving size: 1 cup).

CALORIES 214 (39% from fat); FAT 9.2g (sat 3.9g, mono 3.6g, poly 0.5g); PROTEIN 25g; CARB 7.6g; FIBER 1.1g; CHOL 59mg; IRON 2.8mg; SODIUM 407mg; CALC 17mg

Thai chiles create enough heat to spice up any meal. You may not find these curvy bright red or deep green peppers in the grocery store, but you can usually buy them in Asian specialty markets. Choose Thai chiles that are intense in color and firm to the touch. Cover and store them in the refrigerator up to ten days. Bird chiles from South America are a bit smaller but are just as hot. They are an ideal substitute, but serrano chiles are an easier-to-find stand-in.

You may find this salad listed on menus in Thai restaurants as yam nuea yang, *which means "tossed beef." Featuring grassy cilantro, citrusy lime juice, salty fish sauce, and fiery chiles, this traditional fare offers big taste with minimal ingredients. The salad can be eaten hot or cold. It's often served with jasmine or sticky rice, which is perfect for soaking up the spicy sauce.*

Grilled Steak Salad with Creamy Ranch Dressing

Ranch dressing was created on a dude ranch in Santa Barbara in the 1950s. Its creamy texture and rich, appetizing, and satisfying flavor have made it America's top-selling dressing since the 1990s. The full-fat variety contains a whopping 14 grams of fat per serving. Go with a light or fat-free version to get the taste you love without the fat.

Steak:

½ teaspoon garlic powder
½ teaspoon brown sugar
½ teaspoon ground red pepper
¼ teaspoon salt
¼ teaspoon black pepper
1 (1-pound) boneless sirloin steak, trimmed (about ½ inch thick)
Cooking spray

Salad:

4 (1-ounce) slices sourdough bread
1 garlic clove, halved
2 cups grape tomatoes
1 cup halved and sliced cucumber
1 cup sliced red onion
1 (16-ounce) bag classic iceberg salad mix (such as Dole)
½ cup fat-free ranch dressing

1. Heat a nonstick grill pan over medium-high heat.
2. Preheat broiler.
3. To prepare steak, combine first 5 ingredients, and rub evenly over both sides of steak. Coat grill pan with cooking spray. Cook steak 4 minutes on each side or until desired degree of doneness. Remove from pan; let stand 5 minutes. Cut steak diagonally across grain into thin slices.
4. While steak stands, prepare salad. Place bread slices on a baking sheet, and broil 2 minutes on each side or until lightly browned. Rub cut sides of garlic halves over bread. Cut bread into ¾-inch squares. Combine bread squares, tomatoes, cucumber, onion, and salad mix in a large bowl. Add dressing, tossing gently to coat. Divide salad among 4 plates; top with steak. Yield: 4 servings (serving size: 3 cups salad and about 3 ounces meat).

CALORIES 334 (20% from fat); FAT 7.5g (sat 2.6g, mono 3.1g, poly 0.6g); PROTEIN 29.2g; CARB 37g; FIBER 4.8g; CHOL 67mg; IRON 3.6mg; SODIUM 733mg; CALC 73mg

Sourdough croutons, creamy ranch dressing, and steak seasoned with a sweet-spicy rub make this down-home salad a family favorite. A grill pan imparts grilled flavor without the trouble of firing up the grill.

Pork Fattoush

Pita bread is a round yeast flatbread that is traditional in many Middle Eastern and Mediterranean cuisines. It is used to scoop up sauces and dips, or it can be opened into a pocket for sandwich fillings. Visit a Middle Eastern bakery to find the freshest selection of pita bread; it should be soft and moist. Because pita bread tends to dry out quickly, store it in a tightly sealed plastic bag.

1½ teaspoons bottled minced garlic
¾ teaspoon salt, divided
1 pound pork tenderloin, trimmed and cut into ¾-inch cubes
1 tablespoon olive oil
2 (7-inch) pitas
3 cups chopped tomato
½ cup chopped green onions
⅓ cup chopped fresh mint
1 tablespoon balsamic vinegar
1 teaspoon lemon juice
1 cucumber, peeled, quartered lengthwise, and sliced into ¼-inch pieces
1 (7-ounce) bottle roasted red bell peppers, drained and chopped

1. Preheat oven to 400°.

2. Combine garlic, ½ teaspoon salt, and pork, tossing well to coat. Let stand 5 minutes. Heat oil in a large nonstick skillet over medium-high heat.

3. Arrange pitas in a single layer directly on oven rack. Bake at 400° for 5 minutes or until crisp; transfer pitas to a wire rack.

4. While pitas bake, add pork to pan; cook 5 minutes or until done, stirring frequently. Place pork in a large bowl. Stir in remaining ¼ teaspoon salt, tomato, and next 6 ingredients. Break toasted pitas into bite-sized pieces. Add to pork mixture; toss to combine. Serve immediately. Yield: 4 servings (serving size: 2 cups).

CALORIES 314 (25% from fat); FAT 8.6g (sat 2.1g, mono 4.6g, poly 1.3g); PROTEIN 28.9g; CARB 30g; FIBER 3.7g; CHOL 74mg; IRON 3.4mg; SODIUM 852mg; CALC 62mg

This traditional Middle Eastern bread salad uses toasted pita bread, which adds a dry crispness to the succulent cucumbers, tomatoes, and bell peppers. The dressing typically only includes lemon juice, olive oil, and salt, but we enjoyed the intense, sweet flavor added by balsamic vinegar. You can substitute leftover whole wheat, French, or sourdough bread cut into cubes and toasted for the pita, if desired.

Gazpacho Panzanella

Cutting the croutons for this bread salad is easy if you use a serrated knife. With its scalloped toothlike edge, this knife is ideal for cutting through foods with a hard exterior and a softer interior, such as a loaf of crusty bread. The principle behind a serrated knife is similar to that of a saw: The teeth of the blade catch and rip the crust as the knife smoothly slices through the bread.

Salad:
- 4 (1-ounce) slices French bread, cut into ½-inch cubes
- Cooking spray
- 3½ cups chopped seeded tomato (about 2 pounds)
- 2 cups chopped skinless, boneless rotisserie chicken breast
- 1¾ cups chopped seeded cucumber (about 1 pound)
- 1 cup chopped green bell pepper
- ½ cup vertically sliced red onion
- ¼ cup chopped fresh flat-leaf parsley

Dressing:
- ½ cup low-sodium vegetable juice
- ¼ cup red wine vinegar
- 1 tablespoon extravirgin olive oil
- 1 tablespoon water
- 2 garlic cloves, minced
- ½ teaspoon salt
- ⅛ teaspoon freshly ground black pepper

1. Preheat oven to 350°.

2. To prepare salad, arrange bread cubes in a single layer on a baking sheet. Lightly coat bread cubes with cooking spray. Bake at 350° for 15 minutes or until golden brown, stirring once. Set aside.

3. Place tomato and next 5 ingredients in a large bowl; toss gently to combine.

4. To prepare dressing, combine vegetable juice and next 6 ingredients, stirring with a whisk. Drizzle over salad, tossing gently to coat. Stir in bread cubes; let salad stand 5 minutes. Serve immediately. Yield: 4 servings (serving size: 2½ cups).

CALORIES 294 (24% from fat); FAT 7.7g (sat 1.5g, mono 4.1g, poly 1.4g); PROTEIN 26.9g; CARB 29.6g; FIBER 4.4g; CHOL 60mg; IRON 3mg; SODIUM 553mg; CALC 68mg

This colorful salad combines gazpacho (the classic Spanish soup) and panzanella (the Italian bread salad). Chop the vegetables and toast the bread cubes ahead of time, but toss the salad just before serving; the bread will soak up the juices and become soggy if it sits too long. If you prefer a drier panzanella, simply add less dressing.

White Bean and Roasted Chicken Salad

Salad:

- 2 cups coarsely chopped skinless, boneless rotisserie chicken breast
- 1 cup chopped tomato
- ½ cup thinly sliced red onion
- ⅓ cup sliced fresh basil
- 2 (16-ounce) cans cannellini beans or other white beans, rinsed and drained

Dressing:

- ¼ cup red wine vinegar
- 2 tablespoons extravirgin olive oil
- 1 tablespoon fresh lemon juice
- 2 teaspoons Dijon mustard
- ½ teaspoon salt
- ¼ teaspoon freshly ground black pepper
- 2 garlic cloves, minced

1. To prepare salad, place first 5 ingredients in a large bowl; stir gently to combine.

2. To prepare dressing, combine red wine vinegar and the next 6 ingredients, stirring with a whisk. Drizzle over salad, tossing gently to coat. Yield: 5 servings (serving size: about 1¼ cups).

CALORIES 369 (25% from fat); FAT 10.1g (sat 2g, mono 5.7g, poly 1.7g); PROTEIN 29.2g; CARB 41.5g; FIBER 9.6g; CHOL 45mg; IRON 4mg; SODIUM 342mg; CALC 117mg

For a busy lifestyle, rotisserie chicken is a convenient and delicious solution. Found in the supermarket deli, this juicy precooked chicken makes an easy weeknight entrée on its own, or it can be chopped, sliced, or shredded as an ingredient in a homemade meal. An average 2-pound roasted chicken yields about 3½ cups of meat. Store it covered in the refrigerator for up to four days.

Great for picnics or lazy-day suppers, this salad stirs together in a flash. The classic red wine vinaigrette adds a nice zing to the creamy cannellini beans and roasted chicken. Red onion adds some bite, while basil imparts a subtle hint of licorice and cloves.

Salmon on Greens with Lime-Ginger Dressing

⅔ cup fresh lime juice (about 5 limes)
½ cup honey
½ teaspoon grated peeled fresh ginger
4 (6-ounce) skinless salmon fillets (about 1 inch thick)
Cooking spray
¼ teaspoon salt
8 cups gourmet salad greens
1 cup sliced peeled mango

1. Preheat broiler.
2. Combine first 3 ingredients in a small bowl, reserving ¾ cup juice mixture for dressing. Place salmon fillets on a broiler pan coated with cooking spray, and baste with remaining juice mixture. Broil 4 minutes on each side or until desired degree of doneness, basting once after turning. Sprinkle fillets with salt.
3. Divide salad greens and mango among 4 plates; top with salmon fillets. Drizzle with reserved ¾ cup dressing. Yield: 4 servings (serving size: 2 cups salad greens, ¼ cup mango, 1 salmon fillet, and 3 tablespoons dressing).

CALORIES 462 (28% from fat); FAT 14.5g (sat 2.5g, mono 6.8g, poly 3.2g); PROTEIN 37.2g; CARB 48.3g; FIBER 2.5g; CHOL 111mg; IRON 2.2mg; SODIUM 243mg; CALC 60mg

To prevent contamination, make sure to set aside ¾ cup of the juice mixture for the dressing before basting the raw salmon. Any of the mixture that is left over from the basting should be discarded. Never reuse marinade that has been used to marinate or baste raw meat or fish unless you boil it first for 1 minute.

Transform a simple broiled salmon fillet into a one-dish meal by serving it over gourmet greens with fresh mango and adding a sweet, spicy dressing. Keep individually-packed frozen salmon fillets on hand so that you can put this salad together without making a trip to the fish market.

Salade Niçoise with Creamy Tofu Dressing

For the perfect hard-cooked eggs, place eggs in a single layer in a saucepan with just enough cool water to cover them by 1 inch. Cover the pan, and bring the water just to a boil; immediately turn off the heat. Let the eggs stand, covered, for 15 minutes. Run the eggs under cold water until completely cooled. Gently crack each shell, and peel under running water, starting with the large end. Use older eggs because eggs older than seven days are easier to peel.

Dressing:
- 1 tablespoon water
- 1 tablespoon red wine vinegar
- 1 tablespoon fresh lemon juice
- 1 teaspoon chopped fresh thyme
- ¼ teaspoon salt
- ¼ teaspoon freshly ground black pepper
- 4 ounces firm silken tofu
- 2 canned anchovy fillets
- 1 garlic clove, chopped

Salad:
- 12 ounces small red potatoes
- 12 ounces green beans
- 1½ pounds fresh tuna
- ½ teaspoon salt
- ¼ teaspoon freshly ground black pepper
- Cooking spray
- 1 cup thinly sliced red onion, separated into rings
- 2 tomatoes, each cut into 12 wedges
- 1 hard-cooked large egg, cut into 6 wedges
- 2 tablespoons chopped fresh flat-leaf parsley
- 1 tablespoon capers
- 24 green picholine or niçoise olives

1. To prepare dressing, place first 9 ingredients in a food processor or blender; process 1 minute or until smooth. Cover and chill.

2. To prepare salad, place potatoes in a saucepan; cover with water. Bring to a boil. Reduce heat; simmer 10 minutes or until tender. Drain and rinse with cold water. Drain and cut potatoes in half. Set aside.

3. Cook beans in boiling water 3 minutes or until crisp-tender. Drain and rinse with cold water; drain. Set aside.

4. Prepare grill or preheat grill pan.

5. Sprinkle fish with ½ teaspoon salt and ¼ teaspoon pepper. Place fish on grill rack or grill pan coated with cooking spray; cook 4 minutes on each side or until fish is medium-rare or desired degree of doneness. Break fish into large chunks. Arrange fish, beans, and onion in center of a large serving platter; arrange potato halves, tomato, and egg around fish mixture. Sprinkle with parsley, capers, and olives. Drizzle with dressing. Yield: 6 servings (serving size: 4 ounces tuna, ½ cup beans, about 3 onion rings, about 5 potato halves, 4 tomato wedges, 1 egg wedge, 4 olives, ½ teaspoon capers, and about 2 tablespoons dressing).

CALORIES 276 (29% from fat); FAT 9g (sat 2g, mono 3.6g, poly 2.3g); PROTEIN 30.8g; CARB 18.3g; FIBER 4g; CHOL 78mg; IRON 3.1mg; SODIUM 781mg; CALC 69mg

Of French origin, salade niçoise traditionally includes crisp vegetables, hard-boiled eggs, tuna, anchovies, and olive oil. We've updated it with a tofu dressing. If you're not an anchovy fan, omit them and add one tablespoon of drained capers to the dressing.

Coconut, Crab, and Shrimp Salad

Cooking spray
½ pound medium shrimp, peeled and deveined
½ teaspoon salt, divided
1 cup fresh (about 2 ears) or frozen corn kernels, thawed
⅓ cup finely chopped onion
⅓ cup chopped fresh cilantro
⅓ cup diced peeled avocado
½ pound lump crabmeat, drained and shell pieces removed
1 jalapeño pepper, seeded and chopped
3 tablespoons fresh lemon juice
2 teaspoons extravirgin olive oil
6 cups torn Boston lettuce (about 3 small heads)
¼ cup flaked sweetened coconut, toasted

1. Heat a medium nonstick skillet over medium-high heat; coat pan with cooking spray. Add shrimp and ¼ teaspoon salt; cook 4 minutes or until shrimp are done, turning once. Remove from pan. Coarsely chop shrimp.

2. Combine corn and next 5 ingredients in a medium bowl. Gently stir in shrimp.

3. Combine lemon juice, oil, and remaining ¼ teaspoon salt, stirring with a whisk. Drizzle juice mixture over shrimp mixture; toss gently to coat. Divide lettuce among 4 plates; top with shrimp mixture. Sprinkle with coconut. Yield: 4 servings (serving size: 1½ cups lettuce, about 1 cup shrimp mixture, and 1 tablespoon coconut).

Note: To avoid using two pans, toast the coconut over medium-high heat until golden before cooking the shrimp.

CALORIES 223 (34% from fat); FAT 8.5g (sat 2.2g, mono 3.6g, poly 1.3g); PROTEIN 24g; CARB 16g; FIBER 3g; CHOL 124mg; IRON 3mg; SODIUM 613mg; CALC 94mg

Canned crabmeat is an economical alternative to fresh lump crabmeat and pasteurized fresh crabmeat, so feel free to use it if you prefer. To freshen the flavor of the canned crabmeat, soak it in ice water for 10 minutes; then drain and pat it dry. Find canned crabmeat on the supermarket aisle along with canned tuna and salmon. Fresh crabmeat and pasteurized fresh crabmeat must be refrigerated. Fresh crabmeat should be used within 2 days of purchase. However, pasteurized fresh crabmeat can be kept unopened for up to 30 days after the purchase date and up to four days after it has been opened.

With the bright colors of corn, avocado, and shrimp, this fresh seafood salad is a feast for the eyes as well as the appetite. Scoop it up with baked pita wedges that are sprinkled with sesame seeds. For a spicier dish, add the jalapeño pepper seeds or use two peppers.

Greek Dinner Salad

Dill is a traditional herb used in Greek cuisine. Since ancient Roman times, dill has been a symbol of vitality. In the Middle Ages, it was thought to provide protection against witches and was used as an ingredient in many magic potions. In the kitchen, its feathery leaves lend a fresh, sharp flavor to all kinds of foods. If you don't have fresh dill, this is an herb that maintains good flavor when it's dried. Substitute 3 teaspoons dried dill for the 3 tablespoons fresh.

¼ cup coarsely chopped fresh parsley
3 tablespoons coarsely chopped fresh dill
1 tablespoon extravirgin olive oil
1 tablespoon fresh lemon juice
1 teaspoon dried oregano
6 cups shredded romaine lettuce
3 cups chopped tomato
1 cup thinly sliced red onion
¾ cup (3 ounces) crumbled feta cheese
1 tablespoon capers
1 cucumber, peeled, quartered lengthwise, and thinly sliced
1 (19-ounce) can chickpeas (garbanzo beans), rinsed and drained
6 (6-inch) whole wheat pitas, each cut into 8 wedges

1. Combine first 5 ingredients in a large bowl; stir with a whisk. Add lettuce and next 6 ingredients; toss well. Serve with pita wedges. Yield: 6 servings (serving size: 2 cups salad and 8 pita wedges).

CALORIES 388 (29% from fat); FAT 14.8g (sat 3.8g, mono 4.8g, poly 1.4g); PROTEIN 15.7g; CARB 64.9g; FIBER 11.4g; CHOL 17mg; IRON 4.8mg; SODIUM 779mg; CALC 173mg

This main-dish salad features traditional Greek ingredients, such as olive oil, lemon juice, oregano, cucumbers, tomatoes, and feta. However, it's also delicious if you try some variations—change the fresh herbs, beans, and cheese to use what you have on hand. For a heartier salad, add grilled chicken breast strips.

grain & pasta salads

Barley "Pasta" Salad

English cucumbers naturally have fewer seeds than regular cucumbers. Because there's no need to seed them, they can be prepared faster. Of course, any garden-variety cucumber will make a fine substitution in a recipe that calls for English cucumbers—you'll just have to seed them (for instructions, see page 124). You can find English cucumbers in most major grocery stores, but they're more expensive than their common kin. They're also bigger, and they usually come individually wrapped in plastic.

2 cups water
½ cup uncooked pearl barley
2 tablespoons fresh lemon juice
1 tablespoon olive oil
½ teaspoon salt
2 cups finely chopped seeded tomato
1 cup thinly sliced spinach
½ cup finely chopped green bell pepper
½ cup chopped peeled English cucumber
½ cup (2 ounces) diced part-skim mozzarella cheese
¼ cup finely chopped pepperoncini peppers
2 teaspoons dried oregano

1. Bring 2 cups water to a boil in a large saucepan. Add barley; cover, reduce heat, and simmer 45 minutes. Drain and rinse with cold water; drain.

2. Combine lemon juice, oil, and salt in a large bowl; stir well with a whisk. Add barley, tomato, and remaining ingredients, and toss gently to coat. Yield: 5 servings (serving size: about 1 cup).

CALORIES 153 (31% from fat); FAT 5.2g (sat 1.6g, mono 2.6g, poly 0.6g); PROTEIN 6g; CARB 22.4g; FIBER 5g; CHOL 7mg; IRON 1.8mg; SODIUM 436mg; CALC 107mg

Olive oil, tomato, bell pepper, cucumber, and cheese are common ingredients in a pasta salad, but we replaced the pasta with fiber-rich barley. This salad travels well and makes a tasty to-go lunch. Feel free to add or take out veggies to suit your taste.

Layered Tabbouleh

Bulgur comes from wheat berries (kernels of wheat) that have been steamed, dried, and then cracked. It comes in three types of grinds—coarse, medium, and fine. Medium-grind is an all-purpose size that's good for salads (like this tabbouleh), soups, stews, and multigrain baked goods, as well as meatless burgers and chili. You can find bulgur at most supermarkets or in Middle Eastern markets and natural-food stores.

1 cup uncooked medium bulgur
¾ cup fresh lemon juice (about 4 large lemons)
2 tablespoons extravirgin olive oil
1¾ teaspoons salt, divided
3 garlic cloves, minced
2 cups finely chopped red onion
5 cups chopped tomato
½ cup chopped fresh parsley
½ cup chopped fresh mint
¼ cup chopped fresh dill
2 cups chopped seeded peeled cucumber
1 cup chopped red bell pepper
¼ teaspoon freshly ground black pepper

1. Place bulgur in a large bowl. Combine lemon juice, oil, 1 teaspoon salt, and garlic in a small bowl; stir well with a whisk. Drizzle juice mixture over bulgur.

2. Layer onion, tomato, parsley, mint, dill, cucumber, and bell pepper evenly over bulgur mixture. Sprinkle with remaining ¾ teaspoon salt and black pepper. Cover with plastic wrap; refrigerate at least 24 hours or up to 48 hours. Toss salad well before serving. Yield: 8 servings (serving size: 1 cup).

CALORIES 148 (26% from fat); FAT 4.2g (sat 0.6g, mono 2.6g, poly 0.6g); PROTEIN 4.3g; CARB 26.9g; FIBER 6.1g; CHOL 0mg; IRON 1.6mg; SODIUM 532mg; CALC 40mg

Make this traditional Lebanese salad at least a day ahead so the bulgur has time to soften and absorb the lemon juice. Serve chilled or at room temperature along with grilled lamb or chicken. It's also a good choice for potluck suppers and picnics.

Cuban Beans and Rice Salad

½ cup diced peeled avocado
2 tablespoons balsamic
   vinegar
1 tablespoon olive oil
1 teaspoon ground cumin
½ teaspoon salt
¼ teaspoon black pepper
3 cups cooked white rice
1 cup chopped seeded plum
   tomato (about 3 tomatoes)
¼ cup minced fresh parsley
1 (15-ounce) can black beans,
   rinsed and drained
2 tablespoons minced fresh
   cilantro (optional)

1. Combine first 6 ingredients in a bowl, and toss gently. Add rice, next 3 ingredients, and cilantro, if desired; toss well. Serve chilled or at room temperature. Yield: 6 servings (serving size: 1 cup).

CALORIES 184 (23% from fat); FAT 4.6g (sat 0.7g, mono 3g, poly 0.5g); PROTEIN 4.9g; CARB 32.8g; FIBER 4g; CHOL 0mg; IRON 2.3mg; SODIUM 421mg; CALC 36mg

Cumin is an aromatic member of the parsley family with a pungent, nutty flavor. Its earliest recorded use comes from ancient Greece, and it is still used in many Mediterranean dishes. It also appears in Indian curries and garam masala, Mexican chili powders and salsa, Thai marinades, North African Berber spice mixes, and European sausages. In this dish, it takes on a Latin-American role. Cumin is typically found ground, but you can also buy the seeds whole.

This recipe can be prepared quickly and is a great side for a barbecue or picnic. Use leftover white rice if you have it.

Spelt Salad with Fava Beans

1 cup uncooked spelt or wheat berries

4 cups water

2 cups shelled unpeeled fava beans (about 2 pounds whole pods)

½ cup chopped drained oil-packed sun-dried tomato halves

½ cup diced celery

⅓ cup dried currants

3 tablespoons balsamic vinegar

1 tablespoon extravirgin olive oil

½ teaspoon salt

½ teaspoon freshly ground black pepper

2 garlic cloves, crushed

¼ cup chopped fresh parsley

1. Place spelt in a large saucepan; cover with water to 2 inches above spelt. Bring to a boil. Cover, reduce heat, and simmer 1½ hours or until spelt is tender. Drain.

2. Bring 4 cups water to a boil in a medium saucepan. Add fava beans; cook 2 minutes. Drain and rinse beans with cold water; drain. Remove and discard tough outer skins from beans.

3. Combine spelt, fava beans, tomato, celery, and currants in a large bowl. Combine vinegar and next 4 ingredients, stirring with a whisk. Drizzle over spelt mixture, and toss well to coat. Sprinkle with parsley. Yield: 6 servings (serving size: 1 cup).

CALORIES 190 (22% from fat); FAT 4.6g (sat 0.5g, mono 2.5g, poly 0.5g); PROTEIN 6.2g; CARB 35.4g; FIBER 2.9g; CHOL 0mg; IRON 2.8mg; SODIUM 252mg; CALC 40mg

Spelt is a cousin of modern-day wheat. Once favored by the ancient Romans, it's currently enjoying a comeback among chefs because of its nutty flavor and texture. It has a slightly higher protein content than wheat berries. It's also a good substitute for people with wheat allergies. In addition to this healthful salad, try spelt cooked risotto-style with herbs and spices. Spelt can also be stirred into soups or tossed with beans and roasted vegetables.

This hearty grain salad is full of fresh summer flavors. Once shelled, the fava beans must be removed from their tough outer skins. Blanching the beans makes the skins easier to remove. Just pinch the cooled beans, and the skins will slip off. Lima beans and edamame are good substitutes for the fava beans.

Curried Couscous Salad with Dried Cranberries

Whether fresh, dried, cooked, or made into juice, cranberries are full of health benefits. They contain tannins, which help prevent infection. Tannins are also antioxidants, which neutralize harmful free radicals in the body. Plus, cranberries have a high vitamin-C content. Dried cranberries are a terrific snack and a tasty addition to this couscous salad.

Salad:

1½ cups uncooked couscous (about 1 [10-ounce] box)
1 cup dried cranberries (about 4 ounces)
1 cup frozen green peas, thawed
½ teaspoon curry powder
2 cups boiling water
¼ cup thinly sliced green onions
¼ cup finely chopped fresh basil
1 (15½-ounce) can chickpeas (garbanzo beans), rinsed and drained

Dressing:

⅓ cup fresh lemon juice
1 tablespoon grated orange rind
2 tablespoons water
1½ tablespoons olive oil
1 tablespoon thawed orange juice concentrate
½ teaspoon salt
¼ teaspoon black pepper
4 garlic cloves, crushed

1. To prepare salad, combine first 4 ingredients in a large bowl. Pour 2 cups boiling water over couscous mixture; cover and let stand 5 minutes. Fluff with a fork; cool. Stir in green onions, basil, and chickpeas.

2. To prepare dressing, combine lemon juice and next 7 ingredients in a jar; cover tightly, and shake vigorously. Pour over couscous mixture; toss well to combine. Cover and chill 1 hour. Yield: 8 servings (serving size: 1 cup).

CALORIES 257 (13% from fat); FAT 3.8g (sat 0.5g, mono 2.1g, poly 0.7g); PROTEIN 8.7g; CARB 47.9g; FIBER 4.1g; CHOL 0mg; IRON 2.1mg; SODIUM 243mg; CALC 31mg

With chickpeas, green peas, cranberries, and a zippy vinaigrette, this salad makes a delectable portable lunch. For heartier fare, stir in some chopped cooked turkey or chicken. Make this dish ahead because the flavors meld as it chills.

Chicken and Couscous Salad

The radish, a root vegetable that's a cousin of mustard, provides a crisp, mild zing to salads. Spring is the best season for radishes—those harvested in the summer have a much sharper, almost biting taste. When purchasing radishes, always look for bunches with the leaves still attached. Lively greens are a guarantee of the roots' freshness.

Salad:
1¼ cups fat-free, less-sodium chicken broth
1 (5.7-ounce) box uncooked couscous
1½ cups cubed cooked chicken (about 6 ounces)
½ cup thinly sliced green onions
½ cup diced radishes (about 3 large)
½ cup chopped seeded peeled cucumber
¼ cup chopped fresh flat-leaf parsley
2 tablespoons pine nuts, toasted

Dressing:
¼ cup white wine vinegar
1½ tablespoons extravirgin olive oil
1 teaspoon ground cumin
½ teaspoon salt
⅛ teaspoon freshly ground black pepper
1 garlic clove, minced

1. To prepare salad, bring broth to a boil in a medium saucepan; gradually stir in couscous. Remove from heat; cover and let stand 5 minutes. Fluff with a fork. Spoon couscous into a large bowl; cool slightly. Add chicken and next 5 ingredients; toss gently to combine.

2. To prepare dressing, combine white wine vinegar and next 5 ingredients, stirring with a whisk. Drizzle dressing over salad, and toss to combine. Yield: 4 servings (serving size: 1½ cups).

Note: You can toast the pine nuts quickly in a dry skillet over medium-high heat, stirring frequently. As soon as the nuts become fragrant (about 1 minute after placing them over heat), remove them from the pan.

CALORIES 334 (29% from fat); FAT 10.9g (sat 2g, mono 5.9g, poly 2.1g); PROTEIN 20.9g; CARB 35.8g; FIBER 2.9g; CHOL 39mg; IRON 1.8mg; SODIUM 484mg; CALC 23mg

This salad is delicious and easy to prepare, and the leftovers are tasty chilled. For an extra kick of flavor, sprinkle the salad with feta cheese before serving. If you can't find the specified box size of couscous, you can use 1 cup uncooked couscous.

Roasted Chicken and Bow Tie Pasta Salad

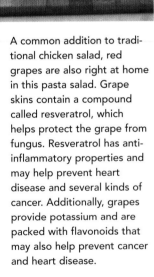

A common addition to traditional chicken salad, red grapes are also right at home in this pasta salad. Grape skins contain a compound called resveratrol, which helps protect the grape from fungus. Resveratrol has anti-inflammatory properties and may help prevent heart disease and several kinds of cancer. Additionally, grapes provide potassium and are packed with flavonoids that may also help prevent cancer and heart disease.

3 cups uncooked farfalle (bow tie pasta; about 8 ounces)
⅓ cup fresh orange juice
¼ cup fresh lemon juice
2 tablespoons extravirgin olive oil
1 tablespoon stone-ground mustard
2 teaspoons sugar
1¼ teaspoons salt
½ teaspoon freshly ground black pepper
1½ teaspoons rice vinegar
2 cups shredded cooked chicken breast (about 2 breasts)
1½ cups seedless red grapes, halved
1 cup thin diagonally cut celery
⅓ cup finely chopped red onion
⅓ cup coarsely chopped walnuts, toasted
3 tablespoons chopped fresh chives
2 tablespoons chopped fresh parsley

1. Cook pasta according to package directions, omitting salt and fat; drain. Cool completely.

2. Combine orange juice and next 7 ingredients in a large bowl, stirring with a whisk. Add pasta, chicken, and remaining ingredients; toss gently to combine. Yield: 6 servings (serving size: about 1⅔ cups).

CALORIES 363 (36% from fat); FAT 14.4g (sat 2.4g, mono 5.5g, poly 4.8g); PROTEIN 18.5g; CARB 42g; FIBER 3.1g; CHOL 33mg; IRON 2.2mg; SODIUM 553mg; CALC 45mg

With a refreshing citrus vinaigrette, crunchy veggies and grapes, and fresh herbs, this is a great light lunch or dinner and an alternative to the traditional mayonnaise-based chicken salad. To cut preparation time, purchase rotisserie chicken from the deli.

Summer Garden Lentil and Pasta Salad

To quickly chop the zucchini for this salad, first cut the zucchini lengthwise into slices. Stack the slices, and cut lengthwise again into strips. Then, keeping the strips piled together, cut crosswise into pieces.

Vinaigrette:

2½ tablespoons balsamic vinegar
1½ tablespoons olive oil
1 tablespoon minced shallots
1 tablespoon Dijon mustard
1½ teaspoons minced fresh garlic
⅛ teaspoon salt
⅛ teaspoon freshly ground black pepper

Salad:

1 cup fat-free, less-sodium chicken broth
½ cup dried petite green lentils
1 bay leaf
2 cups uncooked orecchiette pasta ("little ears" pasta)
1 cup chopped zucchini
1 cup chopped red or yellow bell pepper
¾ cup halved cherry tomatoes
½ cup chopped red onion
2 tablespoons chopped fresh basil
2 tablespoons chopped fresh flat-leaf parsley
2 tablespoons grated Parmigiano-Reggiano cheese
1½ teaspoons chopped fresh or ½ teaspoon dried oregano
1½ teaspoons chopped fresh or ½ teaspoon dried thyme
¼ teaspoon salt
¼ teaspoon freshly ground black pepper

1. To prepare vinaigrette, combine first 7 ingredients in a blender or food processor; process until well blended.
2. To prepare salad, combine broth, lentils, and bay leaf in a saucepan; bring to a boil. Reduce heat, and simmer 25 minutes or until lentils are tender. Drain; rinse with cold water. Discard bay leaf.
3. Cook pasta according to package directions, omitting salt and fat. Drain and rinse with cold water.
4. Combine lentils, pasta, zucchini, and next 10 ingredients. Drizzle with vinaigrette, and toss well. Store in an airtight container in the refrigerator. Yield: 4 servings (serving size: 1¼ cups).

CALORIES 380 (19% from fat); FAT 7.9g (sat 1.6g, mono 4.4g, poly 1.5g); PROTEIN 16.2g; CARB 63.7g; FIBER 7.6g; CHOL 3mg; IRON 3.9mg; SODIUM 447mg; CALC 97mg

Petite green lentils are sometimes labeled "le puy lentils." Other lentils will also work, but the cook time could change, so make sure they're tender before you drain them. Garnish with additional fresh thyme, if desired.

Warm Tortellini and Cherry Tomato Salad

Fresh tortellini is available with a variety of fillings, including cheese, chicken, and mushroom. You can substitute any flavor you like for the cheese tortellini (nutritional information may vary). Look for fresh tortellini in the refrigerated section of your grocery store.

2 (9-ounce) packages fresh cheese tortellini
1½ cups (1½-inch) sliced asparagus (about 1 pound)
3 tablespoons red wine vinegar
1 tablespoon balsamic vinegar
1 tablespoon extravirgin olive oil
¼ teaspoon black pepper
4 cups trimmed arugula
1½ cups halved cherry tomatoes
¾ cup (3 ounces) grated fresh Parmesan cheese
½ cup thinly sliced red onion
⅓ cup thinly sliced fresh basil
1 (14-ounce) can artichoke hearts, drained and quartered

1. Cook pasta according to package directions, omitting salt and fat. Add asparagus during last 2 minutes of cooking time. Drain.
2. While pasta cooks, combine vinegars, oil, and pepper in a large bowl, stirring with a whisk. Add pasta mixture, arugula, and remaining ingredients; toss to coat. Yield: 6 servings (serving size: 1½ cups).

CALORIES 403 (26% from fat); FAT 11.6g (sat 5.7g, mono 4.4g, poly 0.6g); PROTEIN 21.7g; CARB 52.4g; FIBER 7.9g; CHOL 50mg; IRON 1.9mg; SODIUM 725mg; CALC 415mg

Basil, cherry tomatoes, red onion, and arugula bring fresh flavor to cheese tortellini in this satisfying main-dish salad.

vegetable
salads

Warm Asparagus Salad

Rubbing bread with halved garlic cloves is the traditional way to make garlic bread, and the cloves lend a better, fresher garlic flavor than garlic powder. In this recipe, we use this method to make garlic-flavored breadcrumbs.

4 (½-ounce) slices day-old French bread or other firm white bread
1 garlic clove, peeled and halved
1 tablespoon unsalted butter
1 tablespoon white wine vinegar
1 teaspoon grated lemon rind
2 teaspoons fresh lemon juice
2 teaspoons extravirgin olive oil
1 shallot, peeled and minced
¼ teaspoon salt
¼ teaspoon freshly ground black pepper
1 cup water
1½ pounds asparagus
1 teaspoon grated lemon rind (optional)

1. Preheat oven to 375°.
2. Place bread in a single layer on a baking sheet. Bake at 375° for 10 minutes or until toasted. Rub cut sides of garlic over one side of each bread slice. Place bread slices in a food processor; pulse 10 times or until bread is coarsely ground. Arrange breadcrumbs in a single layer on baking sheet; bake at 375° for 5 minutes or until golden brown. Transfer breadcrumbs to a bowl.
3. Melt butter in a small saucepan over medium-high heat. Cook 1 to 2 minutes or until butter is lightly browned, shaking pan occasionally; remove from heat. Drizzle butter over toasted breadcrumbs; toss well to coat.
4. Combine vinegar and next 4 ingredients; stir well with a whisk. Stir in salt and pepper.
5. Bring water to a boil in a large skillet. Snap off tough ends of asparagus; add asparagus to pan. Cook 5 minutes or until tender, stirring constantly. Place asparagus on a serving platter; top with breadcrumb mixture. Garnish with 1 teaspoon grated lemon rind, if desired. Serve immediately with vinaigrette. Yield: 6 servings (serving size: ⅙ of asparagus salad and ½ tablespoon vinaigrette).

CALORIES 94 (36% from fat); FAT 3.8g (sat 1.3g, mono 2g, poly 0.4g); PROTEIN 4.1g; CARB 13.2g; FIBER 0.4g; CHOL 5mg; IRON 3mg; SODIUM 172mg; CALC 37mg

For an outstanding springtime salad, drizzle fresh asparagus with a delicate vinaigrette made of olive oil, lemon juice, and lemon rind. Twice-baked garlicky breadcrumbs tossed in browned butter add a pleasant nuttiness that complements the garden-fresh flavor of the asparagus.

Multibean Salad

2 cups (½-inch) diagonally cut haricots verts (about 8 ounces)
2 cups (½-inch) diagonally cut wax beans (about 8 ounces)
1 cup frozen shelled edamame (green soybeans)
1 cup grape or cherry tomatoes, halved
½ cup finely chopped orange bell pepper
½ cup thinly sliced red onion
2 tablespoons sherry vinegar
½ teaspoon sugar
¼ teaspoon Dijon mustard
2 teaspoons extravirgin olive oil
¼ cup chopped fresh parsley
¼ teaspoon salt
¼ teaspoon freshly ground black pepper

1. Steam first 3 ingredients, covered, 6 minutes or until haricots verts and wax beans are crisp-tender. Drain and plunge beans into ice water; drain. Combine beans, tomato halves, bell pepper, and onion in a large bowl.
2. Combine vinegar, sugar, and mustard, stirring with a whisk. Gradually add oil to vinegar mixture, stirring constantly with a whisk. Stir in parsley, salt, and black pepper. Drizzle vinaigrette over bean mixture; toss gently to coat. Yield: 6 servings (serving size: about 1 cup).

CALORIES 85 (29% from fat); FAT 2.7g (sat 0.2g, mono 1.1g, poly 0.2g); PROTEIN 4.4g; CARB 11g; FIBER 4g; CHOL 0mg; IRON 1.5mg; SODIUM 125mg; CALC 48mg

Edamame (fresh soybeans) are packed with potential health benefits. Each ½-cup serving contains 4 grams of fiber and only 3 grams of fat, all of which is the heart-healthy mono- and polyunsaturated kind. The beans are also high in soy protein, which may help reduce cholesterol when part of a low-fat diet. Plus, edamame is an excellent source of potassium, a mineral that helps prevent muscle cramps by regulating the balance of fluid in the body. Potassium may also help lower blood pressure. Enjoy this sweet, nutty bean in salads for extra crunch and flavor. Edamame also makes a healthy snack.

This updated take on three-bean salad is lower in sodium than traditional bean salads because it uses fresh beans instead of canned. Plus, edamame is a better source of protein than other beans. Try it as a flavorful side to a sandwich in lieu of chips.

Roasted Beet Salad with Tarragon Vinaigrette

With hues ranging from yellow to purple, fresh beets lend themselves to dramatic presentations. Because of their texture, beets hold up well when baked, boiled, or roasted. And because of their sweetness, beets pair equally well with butter or vinegar and citrus. When selecting fresh beets, buy small to medium globes with the stems and leaves attached. They should have firm, smooth skin and no soft spots. To store them, trim the stems to about 1 inch and keep the beets in plastic bags in the refrigerator for up to two weeks. As with all root vegetables, scrub beets well with a vegetable brush to remove any dirt before using them.

  3 pounds golden beets
¼ cup olive oil, divided
  2 tablespoons minced garlic, divided
1½ teaspoons chopped fresh thyme, divided
1½ teaspoons minced fresh tarragon, divided
  1 teaspoon salt, divided
  1 teaspoon black pepper, divided
  1 cup red wine vinegar
¼ cup sugar
  2 tablespoons finely chopped shallots
½ teaspoon chopped fresh oregano
  2 cups vertically sliced red onion

1. Preheat oven to 350°.
2. Leave root and 1 inch of stem on beets; scrub with a brush. Place beets, 2 tablespoons oil, 1 tablespoon garlic, 1 teaspoon thyme, and 1 teaspoon tarragon in a large bowl; toss gently. Place beet mixture on a jelly-roll pan. Bake at 350° for 1 hour or until beets are tender. Drain; cool slightly. Trim off beet roots; rub off skins. Cut beets in half, and place in a large bowl. Sprinkle with ½ teaspoon salt and ½ teaspoon pepper, tossing gently.
3. Combine vinegar, sugar, shallots, oregano, 2 tablespoons oil, 1 tablespoon garlic, ½ teaspoon thyme, ½ teaspoon tarragon, ½ teaspoon salt, and ½ teaspoon pepper in a small bowl, stirring with a whisk. Add vinegar mixture and onion to beet mixture; toss gently. Yield: 8 servings (serving size: about ½ cup).

CALORIES 146 (22% from fat); FAT 3.7g (sat 0.5g, mono 2.6g, poly 0.5g); PROTEIN 3.3g; CARB 26.9g; FIBER 5.3g; CHOL 0mg; IRON 1.8mg; SODIUM 428mg; CALC 43mg

Roasting brings out the natural sweetness of beets, which is balanced here with an herb vinaigrette. While we used rich-colored, golden beets for this flavorful salad, any color of beet will work. Beets tend to bleed, so if you're using more than one color, keep them in separate bowls until you're ready to toss together all the ingredients.

Peanutty Cabbage-Apple Slaw with Raisins

⅓ cup white balsamic or cider vinegar
¼ cup packed brown sugar
1½ tablespoons roasted peanut oil
½ teaspoon salt
¼ teaspoon crushed red pepper
3 cups coarsely chopped Granny Smith apple
½ cup golden seedless raisins
1 (16-ounce) package cabbage-and-carrot coleslaw

1. Combine first 5 ingredients, stirring with a whisk until sugar dissolves.
2. Combine apple, raisins, and coleslaw. Drizzle with vinaigrette; toss well to combine. Cover and chill up to 3 hours. Yield: 8 servings (serving size: about 1 cup).

CALORIES 128 (20% from fat); FAT 2.9g (sat 0.5g, mono 1.2g, poly 0.9g); PROTEIN 1.2g; CARB 26.7g; FIBER 3.1g; CHOL 0mg; IRON 0.8mg; SODIUM 167mg; CALC 40mg

White balsamic vinegar is made with white wine vinegar instead of the traditional red wine vinegar. Because regular balsamic vinegar has a deep reddish brown tint, it will discolor light foods, such as the ingredients used in this salad. The white variety allows these light foods to retain their bright, vibrant colors. White balsamic vinegar is usually less sweet and milder than traditional balsamic vinegar.

In this unique coleslaw, sweet raisins offer a surprising contrast to the crisp, tart Granny Smith apples. A small amount of roasted peanut oil gives this slaw a big hit of flavor with a minimum amount of fat. Be sure that the bottle says "roasted" or "toasted"—it has a much richer taste than regular peanut oil.

Mexican Corn Salad

1 (16-ounce) package frozen shoepeg white corn, thawed
½ cup chopped fresh cilantro
½ cup finely chopped red onion
¼ cup fresh lime juice
2 tablespoons minced seeded jalapeño pepper (about 1 large)
1 tablespoon olive oil
½ teaspoon salt
¼ teaspoon ground cumin
¼ teaspoon chili powder
¼ teaspoon black pepper
2 garlic cloves, minced, or 2 teaspoons bottled minced garlic

1. Combine all ingredients in a bowl; toss well. Cover and chill 8 to 24 hours. Stir well before serving. Yield: 6 servings (serving size: ½ cup).

CALORIES 112 (25% from fat); FAT 3.1g (sat 0.3g, mono 1.7g, poly 0.3g); PROTEIN 2.8g; CARB 19.1g; FIBER 2.8g; CHOL 0mg; IRON 0.2mg; SODIUM 199mg; CALC 8mg

Cilantro, with its distinctive grassy flavor, is the green leaves of the coriander plant, which also gives us coriander seeds. Cilantro is part of the cuisines of Cambodia, India, Mexico, and Israel. It has gained popularity in American kitchens as a key element of Mexican fare. Cilantro has health benefits as well as taste: A tablespoon of cilantro jazzes up a dish while adding less than one calorie and offering a good bit of vitamin A. The best way to distinguish cilantro from fresh flat-leaf parsley is to press a leaf between your fingers. You should quickly detect the more pungent, distinct flavor of the cilantro.

For a quick make-ahead salad that tastes like it's fresh from the garden, toss thawed frozen corn with cilantro, red onion, jalapeño, and lime juice. Serve this salad alongside Tex-Mex fare or at a cookout.

Sweet-Spicy Cucumbers over Tomatoes

Made from the juice of apples (or apple cider), cider vinegar is light brown in color. Although it's still quite sharp, it has a sweeter fruit flavor and is less acidic than most white wine vinegars. Cider vinegar is an excellent every-day vinegar to use when pickling or when preparing salad dressings or barbecue sauces. Unlike other vinegars, which have begotten many gourmet siblings, cider vinegar remains simple and true to its roots. Unadorned cider vinegar is the perfect choice for this classic marinated cucumber salad.

2 cups thinly sliced pickling cucumber (about 2 cucumbers)
1 cup thinly sliced Vidalia or other sweet onion
½ cup cider vinegar
¼ cup sugar
½ teaspoon salt
½ teaspoon mustard seeds
4 garlic cloves, minced
2 whole dried hot red chiles
16 (¼-inch-thick) slices tomato
⅛ teaspoon salt
⅛ teaspoon freshly ground black pepper

1. Arrange half of cucumber in a 9-inch pie plate. Top with half of onion. Repeat layers with remaining cucumber and onion.

2. Combine vinegar and next 5 ingredients in a small saucepan. Bring to a boil; cook 1 minute or until sugar dissolves, stirring occasionally. Pour hot vinegar mixture over cucumber mixture. Cover; marinate in refrigerator 1 to 4 days.

3. Arrange tomato slices on a platter; sprinkle evenly with ⅛ teaspoon salt and black pepper. Remove cucumber mixture from marinade with a slotted spoon; arrange over tomato slices. Yield: 8 servings (serving size: 2 tomato slices and about ⅓ cup cucumber mixture).

CALORIES 32 (6% from fat); FAT 0.2g (sat 0g, mono 0g, poly 0.1g); PROTEIN 0.8g; CARB 7.7g; FIBER 1g; CHOL 0mg; IRON 0.4mg; SODIUM 115mg; CALC 11mg

Make this flavorful salad when summer produce is readily available. Be sure to use pickling cucumbers, which are shorter and thinner-skinned than regular cucumbers. Though four days is the maximum time the cucumbers should marinate, the longer they soak in the vinegar mixture, the spicier and more garlicky they'll become.

Lentil Salad

4 cups water
1 cup dried lentils
⅔ cup chopped onion
1 cup chopped red bell
  pepper
1 cup chopped green bell
  pepper
1 cup chopped seeded
  tomato
⅓ cup sliced green onions
⅓ cup reduced-fat Italian salad
  dressing
2 tablespoons fresh lemon
  juice
½ teaspoon black pepper
1 (2¼-ounce) can sliced ripe
  olives, drained
1 (4-ounce) package crumbled
  feta cheese with basil and
  sun-dried tomatoes

1. Combine 4 cups water, lentils, and onion in a large saucepan; bring to a boil. Cover, reduce heat, and simmer 15 minutes or just until lentils are tender; drain. Rinse under cold water; drain.

2. Combine lentil mixture, red bell pepper, and next 7 ingredients; toss well. Cover and chill at least 4 hours. Sprinkle with feta cheese. Yield: 5 servings (serving size: 1⅓ cups).

CALORIES 268 (32% from fat); FAT 9.5g (sat 3.3g, mono 1.1g, poly 0.4g); PROTEIN 15.2g; CARB 33.5g; FIBER 11.4g; CHOL 17mg; IRON 4.6mg; SODIUM 619mg; CALC 119mg

Within the little lentil lies a powerhouse of goodness. The smallest member of the legume family, lentils contain iron, protein, and virtually no fat. A cup of cooked lentils provides 90% of the recommended daily allowance of folic acid, which is known to guard against birth defects. As for dietary fiber, a mere ¼ cup has 4 grams, which is more fiber than a same-size serving of most fruits and vegetables. Don't overcook lentils or they'll lose their texture.

Crunchy vegetables, salty ripe olives, and tangy feta cheese are ideal companions to mellow lentils in this cool salad. If you prefer, you don't have to seed the tomato—seeding is for appearance only.

Red, White, and Blue Potato Salad

Potatoes boast a tapestry of many tints, tastes, and textures—red, blue, white, and purple; nutty and earthy; starchy, waxy, firm, and creamy. This recipe celebrates the diversity of this tuber. Fingerling potatoes are simply immature long white potatoes. Because they're younger, these "new" potatoes are less starchy than mature long whites. Red-skinned potatoes (almost identical to round white potatoes except for their skin color) are waxy, meaning they contain very little starch. Blue potatoes, which can vary from bluish purple to a darker purple-black, have a nutty, earthy flavor.

2 cups fingerling potatoes, halved lengthwise (about 10 ounces)
2 cups small red potatoes, quartered (about 10 ounces)
2 cups small blue potatoes, halved lengthwise (about 10 ounces)
¼ cup finely chopped red onion
2 tablespoons chopped fresh parsley
1 tablespoon chopped fresh dill
1 tablespoon chopped fresh chives
3 hard-cooked large eggs, finely chopped
¼ cup red wine vinegar
2 tablespoons olive oil
2 teaspoons Dijon mustard
1¼ teaspoons salt
½ teaspoon freshly ground black pepper
1 garlic clove, minced
Parsley sprig (optional)

1. Place fingerling and red potatoes in a saucepan; cover with water. Bring potatoes to a boil. Reduce heat; simmer 15 minutes or until tender. Drain; cool slightly. Place cooked potatoes in a large bowl.

2. Place blue potatoes in a saucepan; cover with water. Bring to a boil. Reduce heat; simmer 10 minutes or until tender. Drain; cool slightly. Add blue potatoes, onion, and next 4 ingredients to fingerling and red potatoes in bowl; toss gently.

3. Combine vinegar and next 5 ingredients. Pour over potato mixture; toss gently to combine. Serve warm, at room temperature, or chilled. Garnish with a parsley sprig, if desired. Yield: 6 servings (serving size: 1 cup).

CALORIES 250 (27% from fat); FAT 7.5g (sat 1.5g, mono 4.4g, poly 0.9g); PROTEIN 6.9g; CARB 39.6g; FIBER 3.9g; CHOL 106mg; IRON 2.7mg; SODIUM 576mg; CALC 36mg

This recipe uses a trio of potatoes, but use all of one type or other varieties if you prefer. If your potatoes are larger than the ones we call for, cut them to a uniform size. Blue potatoes tend to bleed, so cook them separately. If you prepare this dish a day ahead, add the blue potatoes just before serving.

Greek Spaghetti Squash Salad

1 (3-pound) spaghetti squash
5 cups chopped plum tomato
1 cup (4 ounces) crumbled
    reduced-fat feta cheese
1 cup chopped seeded
    cucumber
1 cup green bell pepper strips
¼ cup vertically sliced red
    onion
¼ cup chopped pitted
    kalamata olives
3 tablespoons sherry or red
    wine vinegar
2 tablespoons chopped fresh
    or 2 teaspoons dried
    oregano
¼ teaspoon salt
¼ teaspoon freshly ground
    black pepper
1 garlic clove, minced
Fresh oregano leaves (optional)

1. Pierce squash with a fork; place on paper towels in microwave oven. Microwave at HIGH 15 minutes or until tender. Let stand 10 minutes. Cut squash in half lengthwise; discard seeds. Scrape inside of squash with a fork to remove spaghetti-like strands.
2. Combine cooked squash and next 6 ingredients in a large bowl, and toss well. Combine vinegar and next 4 ingredients, stirring with a whisk. Add to squash mixture, tossing to coat. Cover and chill. Garnish with fresh oregano leaves, if desired. Yield: 8 servings (serving size: 1¼ cups).

CALORIES 100 (37% from fat); FAT 4.1g (sat 1.7g, mono 0.1g, poly 0.5g); PROTEIN 4.7g; CARB 13.8g; FIBER 1.5g; CHOL 5mg; IRON 0.7mg; SODIUM 350mg; CALC 85mg

Cooking the spaghetti squash whole in the microwave saves time. Plus, the fully cooked squash is much easier to cut (versus traditional methods where the squash is cut in half before cooking). Just make sure you allow it to stand the full 10 minutes so that it won't be too hot to handle. Removing the spaghetti-like strands within the cooked squash is easy. Simply scrape the inside of the squash with a fork until no strands remain.

The bold flavor components of a traditional Greek salad—feta cheese, kalamata olives, and oregano—are ideal complements to mild spaghetti squash. This recipe stores well in the refrigerator for one to two days, and it's even better the second day. Serve with beef, lamb, or chicken.

fruit salads

Fruit Salad with Honey-Yogurt Sauce

1 cup vanilla low-fat yogurt
1 tablespoon honey
1½ teaspoons grated lime rind
3 cups cubed fresh pineapple
  (about 1 medium)
1½ cups chopped Braeburn
  apple (about 1 large)
1 cup orange sections (about
  2 oranges)
1 cup chopped peeled
  kiwifruit (about 2 large)
⅓ cup flaked sweetened
  coconut
1 banana, sliced
¼ cup slivered almonds,
  toasted

1. Combine yogurt, honey, and lime rind in a small bowl.
2. Combine pineapple and next 4 ingredients in a large bowl; toss gently. Just before serving, stir in banana. Divide fruit mixture among 6 salad bowls. Top with yogurt sauce, and sprinkle with almonds. Yield: 6 servings (serving size: 1¼ cups fruit mixture, about 2 tablespoons yogurt sauce, and 2 teaspoons almonds).

CALORIES 196 (22% from fat); FAT 4.8g (sat 1.8g, mono 1.7g, poly 0.8g); PROTEIN 4.3g; CARB 37.9g; FIBER 4.7g; CHOL 2mg; IRON 0.9mg; SODIUM 40mg; CALC 111mg

One large banana packs 602 milligrams of potassium, 2 grams of protein, and 4 grams of fiber, making this native of Malaysia a healthy addition to any fruit salad. Select bananas that are slightly green and firm with no bruises. (Don't buy bananas that look gray or dull; they've been refrigerated, which prevents proper ripening.) Let bananas ripen at room temperature. When they turn bright yellow but are still firm, they're perfect for a salad.

Prepare and refrigerate the yogurt sauce up to one day in advance. You can also combine and refrigerate the fruit mixture up to three hours ahead, but slice and stir in the banana just before serving to keep it from discoloring.

Tropical Fruit Salad

2 cups (1-inch) cubed fresh pineapple
1 cup chopped peeled papaya or mango
1 cup sliced peeled kiwifruit (about 3 large)
1 cup red seedless grapes
⅔ cup (¼-inch-thick) slices carambola (star fruit; about 1)
¼ cup flaked sweetened coconut
3 tablespoons honey
2 tablespoons fresh lime juice

1. Combine first 6 ingredients in a medium bowl. Cover and chill at least 30 minutes.

2. Combine honey and lime juice in a small bowl; toss with fruit just before serving. Yield: 6 servings (serving size: 1 cup).

CALORIES 128 (13% from fat); FAT 1.9g (sat 1.3g, mono 0.1g, poly 0.2g); PROTEIN 1.1g; CARB 29.7g; FIBER 2.9g; CHOL 0mg; IRON 0.6mg; SODIUM 14mg; CALC 24mg

Carambola is often referred to as star fruit because its small oval body has five deep grooves running its length; when cut crosswise, it looks like a star. The tropical carambola has a waxy skin that's bright yellow and a sweet to tart yellow flesh that tastes like a combination of lemon, pineapple, and apple. When ripe, the carambola is juicy and fragrant. Choose carambola that are firm to the touch and have an even golden color. Avoid those with green on the ribs.

Feel free to use this recipe as a general guide, substituting your favorite tropical fruit as desired. This is a good salad to pack for lunch or to take to a potluck supper. Just be sure to store the fruit mixture and the dressing separately and toss them together just before serving.

Spicy-Sweet Melon Salad

½ cup sugar
½ cup water
½ small jalapeño pepper, thinly
   sliced
2 cups cubed peeled
   honeydew melon
2 cups cubed peeled
   cantaloupe

1. Combine sugar and water in a small saucepan; bring to a boil, stirring until sugar dissolves. Remove from heat; add pepper. Chill.
2. Combine sugar mixture, honeydew, and cantaloupe in a large bowl. Cover and chill 4 hours or overnight. Serve salad with a slotted spoon. Yield: 6 servings (serving size: ⅔ cup).

CALORIES 104 (2% from fat); FAT 0.2g (sat 0.1g, mono 0g, poly 0.1g); PROTEIN 0.8g; CARB 26.5g; FIBER 0.8g; CHOL 0mg; IRON 0.2mg; SODIUM 11mg; CALC 10mg

Honeydews are muskmelons, a category of melons that also includes cantaloupes, casaba, and Crenshaw melons. Honeydews have smooth skins that start out pale green and ripen to a creamy yellow. The flesh is light green, sweet, and juicy. Honeydews have less aroma and a more delicate flavor than cantaloupes. The peak season for honeydews is June to October, but they are at their best during the cool months of autumn. Buy them ripe because they do not continue to sweeten after they have been picked.

A simple syrup and sliced jalapeño pepper enhance honeydew and cantaloupe with a subtle sweet heat. The longer this salad sits, the spicier it gets.

Melon, Berry, and Pear Salad with Cayenne-Lemon-Mint Syrup

Fresh mint and ground red pepper are the two key ingredients that make the other flavors in this salad sing. The honey-based dressing and the fruits are very sweet when they're together. The clean taste of the mint and a little heat from the red pepper add just the right amount of contrast to make the other flavors pop.

Syrup:

⅓ cup sugar
⅓ cup water
¼ cup fresh lemon juice
3 tablespoons honey
½ teaspoon ground red
    pepper
¼ cup chopped fresh mint
1 tablespoon grated lemon
    rind

Salad:

6 cups (1-inch) cubed
    cantaloupe
6 cups (1-inch) cubed
    honeydew melon
2 cups blueberries
2 cups quartered strawberries
1½ cups (½-inch) cubed ripe
    pear (about 2 medium)
1 cup blackberries
1 tablespoon chopped fresh
    mint
⅛ teaspoon freshly ground
    black pepper
Mint sprigs (optional)

1. To prepare syrup, combine first 5 ingredients in a small saucepan. Bring to a boil; cook 3 minutes or until mixture is slightly syrupy. Remove from heat; stir in ¼ cup mint and rind. Let stand 30 minutes. Strain syrup through a sieve into a bowl; discard solids.

2. To prepare salad, combine cantaloupe and next 7 ingredients in a large bowl. Add syrup; toss gently to coat. Cover and chill 2 hours, stirring occasionally. Garnish servings with mint sprigs, if desired. Yield: 10 servings (serving size: about 1½ cups).

CALORIES 168 (4% from fat); FAT 0.7g (sat 0.1g, mono 0.1g, poly 0.3g); PROTEIN 2.3g; CARB 42.6g; FIBER 3.1g; CHOL 0mg; IRON 0.8mg; SODIUM 37mg; CALC 33mg

This salad will fill you up, satisfy your sweet tooth, and provide valuable nutrients. All of the fruits in this salad, especially the berries, are excellent sources of antioxidants—damage-control warriors that attack the free radicals that contribute to heart disease, cancer, and aging.

Peach Salad with Cumin Dressing

2 cups frozen sliced peaches, thawed
1 cup thinly sliced seeded peeled cucumber
½ teaspoon grated lemon rind
1 tablespoon fresh lemon juice
2 teaspoons minced fresh mint
2 teaspoons honey
¾ teaspoon cumin seeds, toasted and crushed
½ teaspoon salt
¼ teaspoon freshly ground black pepper
½ cup raspberries

1. Combine first 6 ingredients in a large bowl; toss gently. Combine cumin, salt, and pepper; sprinkle over peach mixture. Add raspberries, and toss gently to combine. Serve immediately. Yield: 4 servings (serving size: ¾ cup).

CALORIES 144 (3% from fat); FAT 0.4g (sat 0g, mono 0.1g, poly 0.2g); PROTEIN 1.4g; CARB 36.3g; FIBER 3.7g; CHOL 0mg; IRON 1.1mg; SODIUM 307mg; CALC 21mg

Cucumber may seem like an unusual addition to this fruit salad, but its mild flavor and crunchy texture are nice complements to the other ingredients. When purchasing cucumbers, remember that the smaller the cucumber, the smaller the seeds and the better the flavor. To seed a cucumber, simply cut it in half lengthwise and scrape out the seeds with a spoon.

Frozen peaches work well in this salad—just thaw them and pat them dry with paper towels to remove excess moisture. Frozen berries, however, don't have the same consistency as fresh and are better to use in a recipe where they are cooked or puréed. Pairing a small amount of fresh berries with the frozen peaches makes this salad taste like it was made using only fresh fruit.

Stone Fruit Salad with Toasted Almonds

Apricots, cherries, nectarines, peaches, and plums are called stone fruits because of their hard, rocklike center seeds. They have thin skins that protect their delicate, sweet, juicy flesh. Stone fruits are available during the warmth and sunshine of the summer months.

1 cup sweet riesling or other sweet white wine
1 tablespoon white wine vinegar
1 tablespoon almond oil
¼ teaspoon salt
⅛ teaspoon black pepper
8 cups mixed salad greens
3 plums, sliced
2 peaches, peeled and sliced
2 nectarines, peeled and sliced
2 apricots, peeled and sliced
¾ cup pitted cherries, halved
¼ cup (1 ounce) crumbled goat cheese
2 tablespoons sliced almonds, toasted

1. Heat wine in a medium saucepan over medium-high heat until reduced to 2 tablespoons (about 10 minutes). Remove from heat; stir in vinegar, oil, salt, and pepper.
2. To serve salad, toss salad greens and fruit with dressing. Divide salad among 6 salad bowls. Sprinkle with cheese and almonds. Serve immediately. Yield: 6 servings (serving size: 1¼ cups salad, 2 teaspoons cheese, and 1 teaspoon almonds).

CALORIES 147 (31% from fat); FAT 5.1g (sat 1.3g, mono 2.6g, poly 0.8g); PROTEIN 3.9g; CARB 24g; FIBER 4g; CHOL 4mg; IRON 1.6mg; SODIUM 141mg; CALC 64mg

This salad was inspired by summer's abundance of stone fruits. A white-wine reduction marries the sweet flavors of the fruit to the vinaigrette. Fresh goat cheese adds a savory note.

Strawberry-Kiwi Salad with Basil

¼ cup half-and-half
1 tablespoon sugar
2 tablespoons white balsamic
  vinegar
¼ teaspoon salt
2 cups quartered strawberries
  (about 1 pint)
3 peeled kiwifruit, each cut
  into 6 wedges
2 tablespoons finely chopped
  fresh basil

1. Combine first 4 ingredients in a bowl. Add strawberries and kiwifruit; toss well. Cover and chill 1 hour. Stir in basil just before serving. Yield: 4 servings (serving size: ¾ cup).

CALORIES 90 (23% from fat); FAT 2.3g (sat 1.1g, mono 0.6g, poly 0.4g); PROTEIN 1.6g; CARB 17.8g; FIBER 3.8g; CHOL 6mg; IRON 0.7mg; SODIUM 157mg; CALC 46mg

Kiwifruit has a sweet-tart flavor that perks up a fruit plate or salad. Choose kiwifruit that are heavy for their size and have no bruises. Keep kiwifruit at room temperature until they are soft and ripe; then store them in a plastic bag in the refrigerator for up to one week. To peel kiwifruit, remove the fuzzy skin with a vegetable peeler using a gentle sawing motion. If the fruit is soft and ripe, you can cut it in half and scoop out the flesh with a spoon.

This salad of sweet strawberries and tart kiwifruit can double as a refreshing dessert. The creamy sauce is irresistible—try dipping pieces of angel food cake into it.

Three Kings Salad

You can section the oranges, cut the beets and onions, and make the vinaigrette ahead. Just be sure to store them in separate containers so the colors don't bleed. Assemble the salad up to one hour before serving.

4 navel oranges
1 (15-ounce) can whole beets, drained
3 tablespoons balsamic vinegar
2 tablespoons walnut oil or olive oil
½ teaspoon salt
½ teaspoon black pepper
¾ cup slivered red onion
Pomegranate seeds (optional)

1. Peel and section oranges over a bowl; squeeze membranes to extract juice. Set sections aside, and reserve 1½ tablespoons juice. Discard membranes.
2. Cut beets into wedges. Set aside.
3. Combine reserved 1½ tablespoons juice, vinegar, oil, salt, and pepper in a medium bowl; stir well with a whisk.
4. Divide beet wedges and orange sections among 6 salad plates. Top with onion. Drizzle with vinaigrette. Sprinkle with pomegranate seeds, if desired. Yield: 6 servings (serving size: ⅙ of oranges and beets, 2 tablespoons onion, and 1 tablespoon vinaigrette).

CALORIES 116 (37% from fat); FAT 4.8g (sat 0.4g, mono 3.2g, poly 0.9g); PROTEIN 1.7g; CARB 18.6g; FIBER 4.8g; CHOL 0mg; IRON 0.7mg; SODIUM 363mg; CALC 53mg

This refreshing holiday salad is as flavorful as it is beautiful. The colorful trio of beets, oranges, and red onion represents the three wise men from the Nativity story. Sprinkle the salad with jewel-like pomegranate seeds for an impressive presentation and additional sweet-tart flavor.

Fresh Fig Salad with Crème Fraîche, Mint, and Prosciutto

⅓ cup crème fraîche
1 tablespoon water
1 teaspoon grated lemon rind
2 teaspoons fresh lemon juice
¼ teaspoon salt
¼ teaspoon freshly ground
   black pepper
24 small dark-skinned fresh figs
   (such as Black Mission,
   Celeste, or Brown Turkey;
   about 2 pounds), halved
¼ cup chopped fresh mint
3 very thin slices prosciutto,
   cut into ½-inch strips (about
   ½ cup)

1. Combine first 6 ingredients, stirring well with a whisk.
2. Arrange figs on a platter. Drizzle with crème fraîche mixture. Sprinkle with chopped mint and prosciutto. Yield: 6 servings (serving size: about 1 cup).

CALORIES 169 (29% from fat); FAT 5.4g (sat 3.1g, mono 1.7g, poly 0.5g); PROTEIN 3.2g; CARB 29.8g; FIBER 5.1g; CHOL 14mg; IRON 0.7mg; SODIUM 214mg; CALC 81mg

Fresh figs are available twice a year: The first crop is available from June through July; the second crop arrives in early September and lasts through mid-October. The dark-skinned Black Mission fig (shown above) is by far the most widely available fig, especially in California (where they're grown) and in the Northeast (where figs must be shipped in). Figs are very perishable, so use them as soon as you purchase them, or store them in the refrigerator for no more than two to three days.

The fresh figs' dense texture and delicate sweet flavor pair well with salty prosciutto. Look for crème fraîche—thickened cream with a nutty flavor—near the gourmet cheeses. If your supermarket doesn't carry it, substitute whole sour cream.

all about
Salad

In this Cooking Class, you'll learn the basics of making fresh, delicious, show-stopping salads. Because this cool dish is simple to prepare and often requires no cooking, we focus on the ingredients and equipment you'll need for success.

Salad Tips

Follow these guidelines for salad success.

- **Buy fresh.** A salad depends on the quality of its components, especially when it's a salad featuring raw ingredients. Fresh, in-season produce will yield a great-tasting salad.
- **Wash** all fruits, vegetables, and greens (including prewashed bags of salad greens) thoroughly before using them.
- **Contrast** crunchy ingredients with creamy dressings; vibrant colors with muted hues; and mellow flavors with spicy, bold ones. The best salads have a balance of textures, colors, and flavors.
- **Go light.** Heavy dressings weigh down ingredients; lighter dressings let other flavors shine through.
- **Chill** your salad plates and serving bowl to keep salad greens crisp longer.
- **To make ahead,** choose a salad that's meant to be chilled, such as a gelatin salad, a potato salad, a bean salad, or a coleslaw. Green salads should not be assembled until just before serving, or they'll get soggy. You can chop raw vegetables for salads and store them separately in heavy-duty zip-top bags in the refrigerator for up to two days. Toss the vegetables with the greens and add the dressing just before serving.

You can also make salad dressings ahead and chill them several days. Just whisk before serving. Give an oil-and-vinegar dressing time to return to room temperature before adding it to a salad.

Essential Equipment

- **chef's knife**—With a good chef's knife, you can cut produce quickly and easily. Keep your knife well sharpened. A dull knife is more likely to slip and cause injury.
- **cutting board**—Use a wooden or plastic board that will give slightly under your knife. (Glass cutting boards have no give, and your knife can slip more easily.) Plastic cutting boards should be cleaned in the dishwasher. Sanitize wooden boards by wiping them with diluted bleach.
- **salad spinner**—Use to quickly dry salad greens. Some spinners have lids so that you can use them for refrigerator storage as well.
- **whisk**—Use to blend dressings.
- **Microplane® grater**—Use to shred fresh cheese and grate citrus rind.
- **pepper mill**
- **salad tongs**
- **large salad bowl**
- **cruet**—Use to serve dressing.

Essential Salad Greens

Every salad starts with a base, and—more often than not—that's a bed of fresh greens.
Here's a glossary of all of the greens and lettuces used in this book plus a few more.

Arugula: This peppery green's assertive flavor is widely used in Italian cuisine. It's slightly bitter and has a hint of mustard. The prime season for arugula is spring, when its leaves are tender and less bitter. Spinach makes a milder substitute.

Butter lettuce: Named for its buttery-textured leaves, this lettuce has a slightly sweet flavor. Handle the leaves gently; they bruise easily. Varieties include Boston lettuce and the slightly smaller Bibb lettuce (shown above).

Escarole: The mildest of the endive varieties, escarole has broad bright green leaves that curl slightly. Escarole has only a hint of the bitterness that is characteristic of Belgian and curly endives.

Belgian endive: This endive variety grows in a compact cylindrical shape with a tapered end. Its pale leaves are slightly bitter with red or pale yellow-green tips.

Curly endive: This lettucelike endive has an off-white, compact center and loose, lacy green-rimmed outer leaves that curl at the tips. It has a prickly texture and a slightly bitter taste.

Frisée: A member of the chicory family, this green has slender, featherlike leaves that range from almost white to yellow-green. It has a mildly bitter taste and adds delicate visual interest to a salad.

Iceberg lettuce: This cool, crunchy head lettuce can hold its texture for hours in a heavy dressing, so it's ideal for make-ahead layered salads. When stored properly, it can keep in the refrigerator for up to a week—much longer than its high-end cousins.

Leaf lettuce (green, red, and oak leaf): This variety has leaves that splay from a central root. The most common are green leaf; red leaf, with its distinctive burgundy tinge; and oak leaf, which is so named because its shape is similar to an oak leaf. Leaf lettuce tends to be more perishable than head lettuce.

Mesclun: Often packaged as "gourmet salad greens," this is a mixture of tender, young salad greens, such as arugula, dandelion, frisée, oak leaf, radicchio, and sorrel. In large supermarkets, mesclun is sold loose in plastic-lined baskets or boxes. Customers bag and weigh the amount of greens they need.

Radicchio: Also known as Italian chicory, this bitter pepper-flavored plant has stark white veins and dramatic coloring that ranges from magenta to maroon. Depending on the variety, it can grow in a small rounded head or have narrow leaves that taper. *continued*

All About Greens

Buying: We prefer to use fresh heads rather than bagged greens because the heads seem to stay crisp longer. Choose greens with fresh-looking, brightly colored leaves with no sign of wilting. Avoid any that are spotted, limp, or yellowing. A brown core does not necessarily indicate poor quality. After lettuce is cut at harvest, the core naturally browns as the cut surface seals to hold in nutrients. If buying bagged salad greens, check the expiration date and choose the freshest.

Cleaning: Wash all greens with cold water. Leafy greens like spinach can harbor sand and other debris; to clean, dunk them in a large bowl, pot, or clean sink filled with cold water. The dirt will sink to the bottom while the greens float to the top. Remove the greens by hand, pour out the water, and repeat the procedure until the water is free of debris. Drain greens on paper towels or with a salad spinner.

Storing: Store washed greens in your refrigerator crisper drawer in zip-top bags with a paper towel to absorb moisture; squeeze out air before sealing. Use within a day or two (use firm lettuces, such as iceberg, within a week).

Measuring: When measuring greens, don't pack the leaves too tightly in the measuring cup. Instead, place them in the cup, and lightly pat down.

Romaine: Romaine leaves grow in heads and range in color from dark green outer leaves to a yellowish-green heart in the center. The lettuce of choice for Caesar salads, romaine adds crisp texture to any lettuce mix.

Spinach: Choose spinach leaves that are crisp and dark green with a fresh fragrance. We like baby spinach because its mild, tender leaves are prime for enjoying raw in salads, and there's no need to trim the stems.

Watercress: This member of the mustard family has small, crisp dark green leaves with a sharp, peppery flavor. Pungent-flavored arugula makes a good substitute. If you don't care for the sharp flavor, you can use spinach.

Essential Oils and Vinegars
These two condiments are fundamental to successful salad dressings.
Discover your options in this convenient guide.

Oils

Oil coats the tongue and tempers the acidity of vinegar. And its flavor plays a central role in many salad dressings.

Extravirgin olive oil comes from whole unblemished olives that are cold-pressed (meaning no heat or chemicals are used) to extract the oil within a day after the harvest. All olive oil is high in monounsaturated fats and rich in antioxidants, such as vitamins A and E, but extra-virgin is the best and most flavorful olive oil for salad dressings.

Oil Storage

Oils are sensitive to heat and light. Store them in an enclosed cabinet away from heat and light and use oils within six months after opening.

Canola oil is made from rape seeds. It's a healthful choice, providing omega-3 fatty acids and monounsaturated fats. Because it's very mild, use canola oil in dressings that are chock-full of other flavorful ingredients.

Sesame oil is high in healthful polyunsaturated fat. Dark sesame oil has a very strong taste and fragrance and is often used for a distinct flavor accent, such as in an Asian slaw. Light sesame oils have a deliciously mild, nutty flavor that's wonderful in salad dressings.

Nut oils have concentrated flavor and offer the same health benefits of their nut sources. Some of our favorites for salad dressings are **almond oil** (see recipe on page 126); **roasted peanut oil** (see recipe on page 102); **walnut oil** (see recipes on pages 40 and 130); **pistachio oil**, especially with salads that contain citrus or seafood; and **hazelnut oil**.

Vinegars

The acidity of vinegar provides an ideal complement to the smoothness of oil in a vinaigrette, and it adds depth and brightness to the other salad ingredients.

Balsamic vinegar is a slightly sweet and full-bodied vinegar that has a hint of tartness. Traditionally, it is aged for decades, becoming more

concentrated and syrupy over time.

Vinegars labeled *condimento balsamico* are aged for shorter periods but are still very tasty and are more reasonably priced.

Red and white wine vinegars are very versatile and are essential to have on hand for vinaigrettes. Wine vinegars, like wine itself,

vary in flavor according to the type of grape from which they are made, where the grapes are grown, and how the vinegar is stored and aged. Those that do not refer to a particular wine on the label are often made from undistinguished wine blends or grape juice. These are what you'll usually find in supermarkets and are fine for most recipes.

Vinegar Storage

Vinegar keeps indefinitely when stored tightly capped in a dark place at room temperature. Because of its high acid content, it's an unfriendly environment for bacteria and won't spoil. Vinegar can become murky or cloudy over time, and you may notice sediment in the bottom of the bottle. This is harmless, but if it bothers you, pour the vinegar through a coffee filter to catch the sediment.

Cider vinegar is made from apple cider. It is light brown in color and has a sweeter fruit flavor and a gentler acidity than most white

wine vinegar, though it is still quite sharp. It's ideal for pickling or for using in salad dressings or barbecue sauces.

Rice vinegar is a light-colored, very mild vinegar that's made from fermented white rice. Its subtle sweet-and-sour flavor is suitable to use

in Asian salad dressings and in dressings for cucumber or seafood salads.

Rice wine vinegar is made from fermented rice wines, such as sake and mirin, and it's sweeter than rice vinegar. It provides a sweet-and-sour flavor without the acidic "heat" of a stronger vinegar, such as white wine vinegar.

Sherry vinegar has a sour-sweet flavor with deep notes of oak. The best ones age in oak barrels and have rounded, distinct notes of hazelnut. Sherry vinegar is a great everyday vinegar for salad dressings, especially ones with nut oils.

Essential Salad Dressings

Whisk together one of these outstanding dressings to turn any bed of greens into a gourmet salad.

Honeyed Lemon-Dijon Vinaigrette

This bright, zesty vinaigrette is also a good marinade for fish, seafood, or chicken.

¼ cup chopped fresh dill
¼ cup white wine vinegar
2 tablespoons chopped red onion
2 tablespoons capers
1 tablespoon grated lemon rind
2 tablespoons fresh lemon juice
1 teaspoon salt
4 teaspoons honey
2 teaspoons Dijon mustard
¾ teaspoon freshly ground black
  pepper
½ teaspoon hot pepper sauce
2 garlic cloves, minced
⅓ cup boiling water
¼ cup extravirgin olive oil

1. Place first 12 ingredients in a blender; process until smooth. Add water and oil; process until well combined. Yield: about 1½ cups (serving size: 1 tablespoon).

Note: Refrigerate vinaigrette in an airtight container up to 5 days, and stir well before using.

CALORIES 27 (80% from fat); FAT 2.4g (sat 0.3g, mono 1.8g, poly 0.2g); PROTEIN 0.1g; CARB 1.6g; FIBER 0.1g; CHOL 0mg; IRON 0.1mg; SODIUM 133mg; CALC 2mg

Balsamic Vinaigrette

This intensely flavorful and versatile vinaigrette will keep in the refrigerator for up to one week.

½ cup basil leaves
⅓ cup balsamic or sherry vinegar
⅓ cup finely chopped shallots
¼ cup water
2 tablespoons honey
1 tablespoon olive oil
¼ teaspoon freshly ground black
  pepper

1. Place all ingredients in a blender; process until smooth. Yield: 1 cup (serving size: 1 tablespoon).

CALORIES 19 (41% from fat); FAT 0.9g (sat 0.1g, mono 0.7g, poly 0.1g); PROTEIN 0.2g; CARB 2.9g; FIBER 0.1g; CHOL 0mg; IRON 0.1mg; SODIUM 1mg; CALC 4mg

Roasted Garlic Vinaigrette

Cornstarch, which is commonly used as a thickening agent, gives this vinaigrette body so that it can better coat a salad. Store the remaining vinaigrette in the refrigerator for up to one week.

1 cup vegetable broth
2 teaspoons cornstarch
2 tablespoons red wine vinegar
1 tablespoon extravirgin olive oil
1 teaspoon sugar
2 teaspoons bottled minced roasted
  garlic
¼ teaspoon salt
⅛ teaspoon freshly ground black
  pepper

1. Combine broth and cornstarch in a small saucepan, stirring with a whisk. Bring broth mixture to a boil over medium heat, and cook 1 minute, stirring constantly. Remove from heat, and stir in remaining ingredients. Cover and chill. Stir before using. Yield: 1 cup (serving size: 1 tablespoon).

CALORIES 13 (62% from fat); FAT 0.9g (sat 0.1g, mono 0.7g, poly 0.1g); PROTEIN 0g; CARB 0.9g; FIBER 0g; CHOL 0mg; IRON 0mg; SODIUM 72mg; CALC 0mg

Citrus Vinaigrette

  3 tablespoons fresh orange juice
1½ tablespoons fresh lime juice
2½ teaspoons extravirgin olive oil
  2 teaspoons honey
  1 teaspoon red wine vinegar
¼ teaspoon salt
⅛ teaspoon freshly ground black
    pepper

1. Combine all ingredients, stirring with a whisk. Yield: ¼ cup (serving size: 1 tablespoon).

CALORIES 43 (63% from fat); FAT 3g (sat 0.4g, mono 2.1g, poly 0.4g); PROTEIN 0.1g; CARB 4.7g; FIBER 0.1g; CHOL 0mg; IRON 0.1mg; SODIUM 148mg; CALC 3mg

Raspberry Dressing

Drizzle this tangy dressing over mixed greens or a fresh fruit salad. You can store this dressing in the refrigerator up to one week.

⅓ cup honey
¼ cup raspberry or red wine vinegar
¼ cup plain fat-free yogurt
  1 tablespoon Dijon mustard
  2 teaspoons olive oil
¼ teaspoon salt
¼ teaspoon black pepper

1. Combine all ingredients, stirring with a whisk. Yield: ¾ cup (serving size: 1 tablespoon).

CALORIES 40 (20% from fat); FAT 0.9g (sat 0.1g, mono 0.6g, poly 0.1g); PROTEIN 0.4g; CARB 8.4g; FIBER 0g; CHOL 0mg; IRON 0.1mg; SODIUM 86mg; CALC 13mg

Poppy Seed Dressing

Try this sweet dressing with a simple salad of strawberries and toasted almonds over spinach or romaine lettuce.

  3 tablespoons sugar
  3 tablespoons light mayonnaise
  2 tablespoons fat-free milk
  1 tablespoon poppy seeds
  1 tablespoon white wine vinegar

1. Combine all ingredients in a small bowl, stirring with a whisk. Yield: about ⅔ cup (serving size: 1 tablespoon).

CALORIES 35 (49% from fat); FAT 1.9g (sat 0.3g, mono 0.1g, poly 0.3g); PROTEIN 0.3g; CARB 4.4g; FIBER 0.1g; CHOL 2mg; IRON 0.1mg; SODIUM 38mg; CALC 16mg

Blue Cheese Salad Dressing

Use this as an all-purpose dressing or dip. Try adding chopped anchovies to a portion of the dressing and pouring it over celery stalks.

  1 cup light mayonnaise
  2 tablespoons cider vinegar
  1 tablespoon canola oil
½ teaspoon dried oregano
¼ teaspoon salt
¼ teaspoon freshly ground black
    pepper
  1 (8-ounce) carton fat-free sour
    cream
  1 garlic clove, crushed
½ cup (2 ounces) crumbled blue
    cheese

1. Combine first 8 ingredients, stirring with a whisk. Stir in cheese. Cover and refrigerate at least 3 hours. Yield: 2½ cups (serving size: 1 tablespoon).

CALORIES 34 (74% from fat); FAT 2.8g (sat 0.7g, mono 0.3g, poly 0.1g); PROTEIN 0.6g; CARB 1.4g; FIBER 0g; CHOL 4mg; IRON 0mg; SODIUM 94mg; CALC 17mg

More Essential Dressings

Several of our favorite dressings can be found throughout the book as subrecipes of other salads.

- Basic Vinaigrette, page 10
- Maple-Balsamic Dressing, page 46
- Creamy Caesar Dressing, page 12
- Green Goddess Dressing, page 20
- Chive-Buttermilk Dressing, page 14
  (shown below)

Subject Index

Recipe Index